The Curriculum:
Research, innovation and change

Proceedings of the inaugural meeting of the
Standing Conference on Curriculum Studies

Editors
Philip H. Taylor
Professor of Education
University of Birmingham

Jack Walton
University of Exeter
Institute of Education

Ward Lock Educational

ISBN 0 7062 3365 4 casebound
ISBN 0 7062 3366 2 paperback
This collection © Ward Lock Educational 1973

Set in 10 on 11 point Linotype Pilgrim
by Willmer Brothers Limited, Birkenhead
for Ward Lock Educational
116 Baker Street, London W1M 2BB
Made in England

Contents

Constitution of the Standing Conference on Curriculum Studies

1 The purpose of the Conference is to bring together people from universities, polytechnics, colleges, schools, local education authorities, national and local institutions and organizations to discuss, debate and deliberate upon matters concerning the study of the curriculum and its practical implementation.
2 The programme for each meeting shall be determined by a committee, to be called the Programme Committee, which shall be reasonably representative of the categories of the people noted in 1, and shall be proposed and elected annually by members of the Standing Conference.
3 Membership of the Standing Conference shall be by payment of a fee to be determined by the Programme Committee.
4 The Standing Conference shall issue its proceedings.

Programme Committee 1974

Armstrong, Mr M.	Countesthorpe College, Leicester
Campbell, Mr G. F.	Southampton University School of Education
Grant, Mr M.	St Helier Boys School, Jersey
Hanson, Mr J.	Oxfordshire LEA
Kaner, Mr P.	Maths for the Majority Continuation Project
Langan, Miss K. M.	Parkside Experimental Centre, Prestwich
Litson, Mr J.	Dorset LEA
Morrison, Mr M. W.	Lancashire LEA
Percival, Mr S. W.	(Conference Secretary) Manchester University
Rudd, Dr W. G. A.	(Conference Secretary) Manchester University
Skilbeck, Professor M.	The New University of Ulster
Tulloch, Miss R.	Swanhurst Bilateral School, Birmingham
Vanloo, Mr C. A.	Vincent Thompson High School, Exeter
Wright, Mr D. E.	Educational Development Centre, Birmingham

Ad hoc members:

Taylor, Professor P. H	Birmingham University
Walton, Mr J.	Exeter University

Coopted member:

Nichols, Mrs A.	(Conference Secretary) Manchester University

Introduction

The papers collected together in this volume are the proceedings of the inaugural Standing Conference on Curriculum Studies held at the University of Exter in the spring of 1973. In most, if not all, respects they represent just how far we understand the business of planning, evaluating, innovating, researching into and teaching about the curriculum. But more than this is signalled in their publication. A new organization has been created to foster communication and interaction among all concerned with the curriculum no matter at what level, and to be responsive to their needs.

It was in fact the concern of the group that planned the inaugural meeting that any organization established should serve two major purposes: to bring together people working in different contexts in the educational system in a creative discussion of curriculum issues as they concerned them, and to be responsive to changes in these issues such that no particular view of curriculum problems should persist and predominate unless this seemed in the general view appropriate.

The first purpose was achieved by inviting to the Conference approximately equal numbers of teachers, individuals from local authorities working with schools, and staffs from colleges and universities; and in addition representatives of people from national curriculum agencies and the national inspectorate. The second was achieved by the decision to place the Conference each year into the hands of a freshly elected Programme Committee whose job would be to plan the structure of the next meeting. It is to be hoped that these two principles will continue to guide the membership of future conferences across the ebb and flow of the influences and changes which play upon what is taught in schools and colleges.

By general affirmation those attending the inaugural meeting established the Standing Conference. It was their view that the experience of coming together over curriculum issues of common concern across the range of possible involvement – whether as teacher, administrator, educational philosopher, curriculum developer, teachers' centre leader or university lecturer – was sufficiently worthwhile to warrant support for future meetings. It is in order to foster this judgment that the Standing Conference exists, and in existing will receive continued support only in so far as it continues to provide for a sharing of ideas and insights, and provides for mutual understanding among all those held responsible for what is taught in our society.

Philip H. Taylor
Chairman of the Inaugural Conference

Jack Walton
Secretary of the Inaugural Conference

Toward a Logic of Curriculum Development

PAUL H. HIRST
Professor of Education, University of Cambridge

The purpose of this paper is to elucidate as far as possible the logic of rational curriculum development. It is concerned with making explicit what being rational about such development necessarily entails: that is, to dig out those features which *must* characterize curriculum development if it is to be rational. I am anxious not to express merely a personal opinion on this subject, though there is clearly a danger that I shall end up doing just that. What I am trying to do is to articulate, at least to some extent, what is implicit in the notion of rationally defensible curriculum development. How far I shall succeed in this attempt remains to be seen, but if what I have to say is correct, it can only be denied or ignored at the price of rationality. To be ambitious in this way is, of course, to court disaster. Much of what I say I know will be controversial and indeed all of it may be mistaken. Nevertheless, the attempt strikes me as important, for at present we certainly lack even the beginnings of an adequate account of the logic of this business, and lacking that, we lack also any satisfactory methodology.

One has only to survey the procedures adopted in the curriculum projects at present being developed under the auspices of the major funding bodies, to see that adequate consideration of the demands of rational development is rare and that anything approaching a satisfactory justification of the procedures adopted is hardly ever even attempted. I do not wish to suggest that these projects ought not to be pursued. On the contrary, until we have an adequately expressed account of the logic of the business, we need curriculum projects based on the best pragmatic procedures available. It is reflection on the results of such projects which will help considerably the production of the logic we need. As has often been pointed out, valid deductive arguments existed, and were recognized as such, long before Aristotle explicitly set out their logic in ways that now enable us to readily detect and avoid invalid arguments of this kind. The valid arguments came first, the elucidation of the logic later. In curriculum development too, it would seem likely that the differences between those developments we come to regard as acceptable and those we come to regard as unacceptable, will give us vital clues to the logic of rational procedures.

But there is another approach to this problem, one that seeks, from a clear notion of what a curriculum is, to outline what rational development of a curriculum must involve. It could well be that, by examination of what a curriculum necessitates, and what rational development of these elements entails, using general considerations that must apply to elements of this kind, we can make some progress in elucidating the desired logic. This, at any rate, is what I shall here attempt to do.

In seeking to disentangle this logic, it seems to me necessary to start by stating explicitly what I mean by a curriculum, for only then can we proceed to a grasp of what developing a curriculum might involve. I shall take a curriculum to be a programme or course of educational activities. The use of the term 'educational' might appear too restrictive, in that we might, in some limited sense of that elusive term, consider some curricula to be far from educational. I would be perfectly happy to use the phrase 'learning activities' in my definition instead, provided that this term is also interpreted widely enough. In making use of this definition, I am seeking an outline which will cover the entire scope of current curriculum projects, but one which nevertheless lays down enough terms to make it clear what I am talking about. Certainly, I would like it to be understood right away that the rest of this paper is concerned with curricula defined in these terms only, and therefore one very effective way of rejecting everything I am about to argue would be to reject this starting point – my quite explicitly stipulative definition.

That this definition is radically ambiguous in many ways I know only too well. Let me, however, make it more precise in a number of respects, for I intend it to include certain necessary features of all curricula, and it is these features that matter, not my brief definitional phrase. First, a curriculum, by this definition, is not simply a programme of activities of any kind whatever. The programme of activities of a shop assistant, a factory hand, a dancer, a chef or a truck driver, do not to my mind constitute a curriculum. Why? Because none of these are educational or learning activities. They are not distinguished by the characteristics of curriculum activities.

What, then, is the force of the adjective 'educational' or the adjective 'learning'? Part of it is that curriculum activities have outcomes, they are necessarily marked out by their achievements. If an activity is a learning activity, there must logically be some achievement, intended or attained, by virtue of which it can be described as a learning activity. The same is true of educational activities, for again such activities cannot be distinguished from others without similar reference to the character of their results. Not all activities have results or outcomes in this sense. Some activities can be described in terms of the patterns of movement they involve, patterns which may have no existence beyond the confines of the activity itself. Many other activities however do have products, for example cooking and building, and in these cases the kind of activity involved is only intelligible by reference to the results. Curriculum activities are, I am suggesting, in this class.

Whether these results are best described as outcomes, achievements, ends, aims or objectives, is not relevant at this juncture – what matters here is the recognition that end results are necessary to the description of any curriculum as such. Let me also be clear on another point. I am not saying that the results or outcomes of curriculum activities are prespecified by the teacher concerned, or that either teacher or pupil must be consciously trying to achieve the results. I would simply insist that whoever describes certain activities as constituting a curriculum, thereby sees such activities as producing a particular type of result. The curriculum developer or planner must certainly see things in this way, however the teacher or pupil sees things.

Secondly, I suggest that in a curriculum, the activities are necessarily seen as the means which lead to the results or outcomes. How they bring about the results is at this juncture not my concern. It may be by some sort of deliberate, intentional acts, by accidental, unconscious influence of some kind, or by straight physical causation. My point is that, in a broad sense, what goes on in the programme, however else it may be understood, is seen as producing the results. Once again the best definition for such 'means' is not easily decided on, as the available alternatives seem too restrictive. However, I am not concerned to argue that what leads to the appropriate results is an 'activity', rather than a 'process' or an 'experience'. I shall therefore speak simply of means taken to achieve ends, it being understood that means can take many different forms. Not surprisingly the character of the means usually has much to do with the character of the ends concerned. Once more, I am at present saying only that a curriculum planner or designer must see these activities or processes as means to ends, not that teachers or pupils must also see them as such.

Understood in these means-ends terms, curricula can be the objects of many forms of enquiry and research. In particular, they can be seen in the context of historical developments, and as the products of social forces. Features of a curriculum can, for instance, be related to organizations of knowledge that have arisen from vocational demands or as areas of knowledge legitimated by some social or academic élite. From this point of view, some find it attractive to see curriculum development as entirely the product of historical and social determinism. Such out and out forms of what Karl Popper called 'historicism' hold that all that planners and developers do are simply parts of a whole that must inevitably come to pass. The inevitability thesis may mean that all attempts at deliberate control are so much flotsam on the curriculum sea, or it may mean that the inevitable forces work through the schemes of planners. But whatever its form, rational planning and development only have significance for a historicist if the inevitable course of progress is itself seen as defining the nature of reason. And if that is so, rational planning becomes a matter of the prediction of changes and the facilitating of them. Such an approach to curriculum development, I suggest, is not only based on an unjustifiable doctrine of determinism, but is also fraught with all the incipient dangers of social prediction. This is not the place to rehearse the arguments of Popper and others against different forms of historicism, and in general, curriculum planners have not seen themselves as involved in any such debate. Nevertheless, its favour with curriculum theorists may be on the increase. Certainly, there is an occasional whiff of it in some of the fascinating new work in the sociology of knowledge and the sociology of the curriculum.

In rejecting a historicist view of curriculum development, I am not denying that much of our curriculum practice has simply 'grown' out of its social context, and continues so to develop, without much overt, deliberate planning. But that does not imply that curricula cannot be effectively changed by rational planning. It is true too, that our curriculum planning is at times frustrated by social forces beyond the control of the planner. But if not everything is under our conscious control, that is no ground for assuming that nothing is. Indeed, there is much evidence to suggest that many things are, and that with further knowledge more things will be. The significance for planning of the forces that are not under our conscious control, however, remains considerable, and to this I shall return. For the rest of this paper, I shall take it that in curriculum development we are concerned to produce new curricula in the firm belief that, by careful consideration of the factors involved, we can, by our own actions, change matters in ways we judge desirable.

What then does rational planning involve, when it is a matter of planning the means to a set of educational or learning ends? The classical outline of curriculum planning in these means-ends terms is that set out by Tyler in the 1940s (Tyler 1949). In this, the ends are seen as a set of behavioural objectives, and the means as a programme of learning experiences. His account, though it still seems to hold the field in curriculum theory, has I think rightly been subject to much criticism. Some have objected to his working with a means-ends model at all. It has been argued that curricula are not necessarily planned in this way, that historically they have most frequently not been, and that teachers do not entertain pre-specified ends to which classroom activities are the means. In reply to these criticisms several points must be made. First, no one is going to maintain that any, let alone all, of our school curricula have been rationally planned. Maybe that's just the trouble. The history of curriculum developments is not relevant in this sense to determining what features rational planning will have. Secondly, the fact that teachers do not engage in curriculum activities seeing them as means to ends, or are not necessarily aware of pre-specified ends, is equally irrelevant. What is more important is that anyone who undertakes the rational planning of such activities must view that planning as the determination of means to ends. How participants in the conduct of the curriculum course see what they are doing is another question.

To rationally plan a curriculum, I suggest, does demand an awareness of the ends of the business, and the characterization of such ends is logically prior to the determination of appropriate means. This is a *logical* priority of ends over means I am asserting. It means that rational consideration of a curriculum demands clarification of the ends prior to determination of the appropriate means, for without a grasp of the ends, the significance of the means *as* means cannot be grasped. Of course there is no reason why a curriculum experiment should not proceed along the lines 'Let's try doing so and so and see what happens.' One can, however, only rationally appraise such an experiment, for curriculum purposes, by judging the activities as means to ends that are appropriate for a curriculum.

The major objection to the means-ends approach, however, has arisen from questions as to how one is to specify the ends. Are there not some curriculum activities or processes for which the outcomes cannot be specified? In one sense, maybe so; but in the sense that matters in this context, no. Lawrence Stenhouse has argued that the curriculum is sometimes appropriately specifiable only in terms of the content with which one is concerned and not the outcomes (Stenhouse 1970–1). One may, for instance, be able to say that one is concerned with Shakespeare's *Hamlet* but not be able to say what specifically is to come out of one's concern with the play. To the obvious reply that the outcome is a knowledge, understanding or appreciation of the play, he counters with doubt as to whether these outcomes can be specified in behavioural terms. Again, one can specify the stimulus or input by identifying the work of art or experience to which students are to be exposed, but their response is necessarily individual. Stenhouse grants that there are canons by which the appropriateness of the student's response can be judged and by which understanding and mis-understanding can be distinguished, but he considers these canons unsuitable as ways of describing the outcomes. He also regards them as un-analysable into pre-specifiable student behaviours. In a similar way, Eisner has suggested that we might sometimes be better identifying curriculum activities by the kinds of encounter they involve (Eisner 1969). The outcomes of these encounters can be subjected to criticism, much as, say, an art critic criticises a painting. What one cannot appropriately do is pre-specify what the outcomes ought to be.

These contentions, that curriculum activities can be rationally planned without the specification of the outcomes by the planner, seem to me to gain their plausibility from too restricted a concept of what sorts of things outcomes can be and the appropriate ways of specifying them. Acceptance of a means-ends logic of the kind I have been outlining in no way commits one to a doctrine of the behavioural character of the ends. Nor does it mean that outcomes which are specifiable only as anything that satisfies a set of critical principles or canons are inadequate. The kinds of curriculum activities a planner envisages, using say *Hamlet* as a content, are surely limited by a concept of what sorts of outcomes are desirable, and appropriate activities are planned accordingly. At the next stage, the planner may pursue further outcomes, perhaps as a result of applying certain critical procedures. But these procedures are advocated only because of their significance in relation to the further outcomes now intended. If they are not so related to outcomes, I fail to see how the application of the criticism can be viewed educationally or as part of a curriculum. There may be no unique specification of discreet items of behaviour for the outcomes, but why should that kind of specification be necessary? Ends can be specified in enormously varied ways, some specific, some general, some behavioural, some not. Clear specification of the outcomes, according to their nature, is what is wanted, and sometimes that may well be in terms of the critical canons involved.

Attempts to get away from stating curriculum outcomes or ends can, I suggest, only vitiate rational planning. Either the attempt will succeed and the planning will be irrational, or the ends will be smuggled in but in an ill-considered way. Stenhouse's own attempt begins with the need for planners:

1 to define the value positions embodied in the curriculum specification,
2 to specify a curriculum in terms of content, materials and
methods, to spell out what kinds of classroom activity it stands for
and to define the most critical observations which reveal whether
the specification is or is not being met in any given classroom.
And further:
3 to list and test hypotheses regarding the effects of successfully
realizing the specification and perhaps of failing to realize it in
circumstances which are likely to arise in practice.

In so far as these somewhat elusive demands are to be adequate
for curriculum planning, it seems to me they will necessitate a
concern for the ends which are the objectives of the whole business,
for only in this way can one specify the activities or assess them
significantly. To state one's 'values' is one way of stating the
outcomes. To outline 'methods' is to see activities as producing
outcomes. To assess 'effects' is surely in part to assess actual outcomes against those desired. Unfortunately this approach seems to
me (a) to permit the explicit specification of ends in too vague a
way, merely in terms of a set of values, and (b) to be concerned
much too much with the articulation of different kinds of activities
without grasping firmly their status as being the means to clearly
specified ends.

There is a further point of some importance to be made about the
necessity of the means-ends approach to rational curriculum
planning. It has been described as setting up an engineering model,
or production model, for the curriculum. Why, it is said, cannot
curriculum activities be seen on the analogy of a process of growth,
or as the creation of a work of art? Are these not also processes or
activities that have outcomes of a particular character? If we looked
at the curriculum in these ways, rather than as the process of a
production line, might we not be a little nearer the mark? My reply
is that I am *not* concerned with the production line analogy or
model, any more than with that of growth or that of aesthetic
creation. Indeed I am interested in none of these things and I regard
this kind of search for a model as thoroughly misleading. In
engineering, growth and aesthetic creation, there are outcomes of
various kinds of processes. What is involved in each process is
dependent on the character of the outcome and in each case the
process is radically different. To conceive of one of these cases as a
model for another, is simply asking for trouble. Likewise in the case
of the curriculum. As I have been labouring to point out the
outcomes are here of a particular, distinctive kind, and the curricu-

lum activities – processes, means, call them what you will – must be seen in relation to these. No model has been built into the means-ends approach. Whether that means-ends relationship, as I have for convenience called it, is an engineering production relationship or one of growth or aesthetic creation has not been pre-supposed at all. In fact I think it none of these things. What it is will become apparent from looking at the kinds of things curriculum outcomes are in their own right, and seeing then how these can be achieved. Nothing but confusion can come from seeing this approach in engineering, growth, aesthetic or any other alien terms.

Unfortunately to my mind, Tyler and his followers have indeed led many of those who see the necessity for a means-ends approach to planning, into using the engineering model. Instead of looking at curriculum outcomes in their own right, and carefully examining their character, a dogmatic view of that character has been promulgated, usually summarized in the phrase 'behavioural objectives'. On a radical behaviourist account, curriculum outcomes are entirely changes in observable behaviour, and it is but a step then to seeing them as brought about by scientific and technological planning of the engineering kind. But if the outcomes with which we are concerned in a curriculum are examined in their own right, they will be seen to be forms of personal development of great diversity. We are concerned with people having concepts of a wide variety, knowing facts, having physical and intellectual skills, having certain values and character traits, responding emotionally in appropriate ways, and so on. Each of these outcomes labels what I shall refer to as a 'personal state' of some kind. Of course, both psychologists and philosophers have from time to time regarded these so called 'states' as reducible to certain patterns of observable behaviour. But the heyday of such theories is surely now long past, and we must eschew the errors of this reduction whilst recognizing the important kernel of truth it was seeking to express.

Practically none of the personal states we are interested in can be properly understood simply as a pattern of observable behaviour. In particular, terms like understanding, believing, knowing, judging, are not labels for forms of behaviour, but denote states of mind which are not reducible to the physical. No account in physical terms alone can give us what we are talking about. What is true, however, from an examination of the logic of such concepts, is that the criteria for the existence of such states are expressible in terms of what is observable. A person's beliefs are in fact not necessarily detectable from his behaviour, even under the most critical examination. Achieving a particular belief is not a matter of achieving a particular set of behaviour patterns. His behaviour is always compatible with a vast range of alternative beliefs, some of which are mutually contradictory. Nevertheless, his behaviour is the only basis we have for judging what he believes. The doctrine of behavioural objectives thus frequently runs into one or other of two gross confusions. First, that of taking curriculum outcomes actually to be patterns of observable behaviour. Secondly, if that error is avoided, taking observable behaviour to give us necessary and sufficient criteria for saying the outcomes are achieved. They can give us sufficient criteria for attributing states of mind, but not necessary ones. The first of these errors is likely to distort our whole conception of the means, processes or activities, that a curriculum must involve, for it directs attention to a false notion of the nature of the ends. The second error leads to excessively simple ideas as to how we can know that any particular set of outcomes is achieved.

It must be plain from these remarks, that to my mind our grasp of curriculum planning must be based on a most careful characterization of the nature of the outcomes, by an examination of them for what they are. Only then can we begin to sort out the character of the means for reaching them. Taking the outcomes to be behavioural distorts their character and lands us right in the hands of those who then validly complain that we are planning on a restrictive engineering model.

How then are we to specify the outcomes? Surely by using the terms we have for them already. The items of knowledge we want, the attitudes, values, skills, habits and so on. But are not many of these far too general and elusive for specific planning to take place? Certainly they are. We need to break these descriptions down into patterns of more specific descriptions so as to remove ambiguity whenever we are aware of it. No statement of outcomes is above critical examination in this respect. But can we not lay down some general rules about the degree of specificity that rational planning necessitates? In general, I think the answer is no. If x is a possible outcome, it may be possible in some cases to say that this is a complex built out of outcomes a, b, c, d, ... But any such analysis must terminate somewhere. What a complete set of the logical simples, out of which all the outcomes we are interested in are composed, would look like, we just do not know. A complex outcome, p, might be seen to include a more simple outcome q; but what it involves over and above q, may not immediately be discernible. Indeed, how far an analysis into simples can in fact ever be undertaken is not clear. All we can do, whenever possible, is to work with our ever increasing capacity to understand the character of these ends, using as specific whatever characterization of the elements as is available. What we want for curriculum planning is

17

not so much a taxonomy of outcomes which sets out classes of these in some order of generality, but a mapping of the actual outcomes we are interested in, showing how these relate in detail to others that are more specific, more general, or at the same logical level, those of a different logical character, and so on. Though for limited areas this can indeed be done in part, granted the great diversity of kinds of objectives, and granted too the immensely complex character of the logical relations such objectives involve, the idea of an overall, total map strikes me as an impossible dream. Certainly even the vaguest outlines of such a map exist only in restricted areas. Yet with these we must work as best we can.

But can we not say that rational planning necessitates the specifying of objectives or outcomes at least down to the level of being clear about their behavioural criteria? I think this, in one sense, is true and this is the truth behind the cry for behavioural objectives. The point is not that only when we know these criteria do we know what the outcome is, but rather that only when we know the criteria can we begin to judge whether our curriculum activities are any good. Without clarity about the behavioural aspects we may know perfectly well what we are after, perhaps because we enjoy that state of mind or have that intellectual skill ourselves. But we must be clear about the behavioural criteria if we are ever to judge another person's state of mind in this respect. It is therefore the demand in rational planning for judging the results of curriculum activities, that necessitates clarity about related behaviour. Being clear and specific about the outcomes for which one is planning the activities, does not necessitate such clarity about behavioural criteria. If one has sorted out the behavioural criteria that are relevant, one will surely also have a specific enough grasp of the outcomes one wants for all the demands of planning the activities to reach these. Nevertheless, the level of specificity needed in the objectives or outcomes is, I suggest, a matter of practical judgment, depending on the nature of these outcomes, the educational level of the pupils, their experience of educational activities, the methods being used, etc.

I have spent much time elaborating the logical demands curriculum planning makes for the setting up of outcomes and a proper understanding of their character. But if the planning is to be rational, there must be a reasoned defence for selecting one set of possible outcomes rather than another. Unfortunately at this point too, the traditional Tyler model can be very misleading. In his writings, Tyler himself has repeatedly referred to the *sources* of objectives in the learners' needs, both in contemporary life and in academic specialisms. He sees suggestions from these needs as 'filtered' by means of a philosophical critique and certain psychological principles, so as to provide a selection of objectives for the curriculum. From the point of view of rational planning however, one needs to sharply distinguish the *source* of the objectives of a curriculum from their *justification*. How certain objectives come to be thought up is of itself no guarantee that their inclusion is justifiable. Possible objectives are legion, and what any rational proposal must do is to defend choosing these objectives rather than some other set.

To decide on the objectives by consulting teachers, academics, pupils or anyone else may be an interesting way of going about things, but why should their offerings be the best? And I do mean the best, for the problem of rational choice is not that of choosing desirable outcomes, that is no problem, it is the problem of choosing the best, the most valuable. Deciding here involves making many difficult practical judgments, for one set of objectives can only be defended against another on philosophical, psychological, social, academic, practical or other grounds. What a particular group of people opt for is likely to be based on some relevant grounds, but in general these are likely to be inadequate. I find it unsatisfactory, for instance, that Peter McPhail in his 'Lifeline' project should seek to set up the objectives of moral education from statements by pupils of their needs (McPhail 1972). Not that these were uninfluenced by the project's approach. Indeed the questions to pupils strongly determined the areas of issues pupils offered and of these not all were acceptable to the moral aims built into the project by the officers themselves. But this is an odd procedure if one is after a rationally defensible set of objectives for moral education. What the objectives of moral education ought to be surely cannot be adequately determined by these means. Of course one might, for many reasons, wish to experiment with a curriculum having these objectives. Its motivational character is of major interest, for example. But of itself the curriculum that results lacks proper defence. What I'm saying is simply that it is not the sources of the objectives that matters in rational planning, it is their justification as ends.

But granted we have a set of justifiable outcomes, rational planning next demands attention to the means, that is the course or programme of learning activities. How is one to decide on this? Can we, from a set of objectives, make any inferences about the means to achieving these? In any grand over-all sense, no, we cannot, but in detail maybe we can. After all, the outcomes we are interested in are vastly different in character, from say, having a grasp of the Christian concept of salvation, to say, being honest, or being able to swim. Any generally valid inferences about the means to reaching these ends are therefore most unlikely. But at a more specific level there is perhaps hope. For instance, being the type of beings we are, complex abstract concepts can only be grasped in certain ways. Maybe there is a variety of approaches to such concepts but maybe they all must include certain activities or experiences. Could the concept of salvation be understood without a great deal of moral understanding? And what in turn does that necessitate? A similar approach could be applied to acquiring a moral or a physical disposition, though the character of the necessary elements will differ radically between these cases. Do all physical skills *have* to be learnt by practice? If so, what sort of practice exactly?

Whether these demands are logical or empirical necessities is a difficult question which, from a practical point of view, may not be all that important. What is important, is that if we go at the matter carefully in particular cases, using all the forms of logical analysis and empirical enquiry available, we might well be able to determine much more about these processes. In a similar vein, Gagné has proposed a pattern of task analysis which, stage by stage, works backwards from the outcome wanted by asking at each stage what a learner would have to know already in order to arrive at this stage, granted a particular learning task is to be used (Gagné 1965). Hypotheses about learning stages and their relations are, he argues, susceptible to empirical test. Maybe not all outcomes can be approached in this way, but no matter, maybe many can.

There is another way too in which the outcomes themselves would seem to determine, to a large extent, the means to them. So far I have assiduously refused the demand that in a curriculum, the outcomes or objectives are consciously aimed at by the teachers involved, as they plan learning activities for the pupils. I have insisted only that the curriculum planner must be conscious of the outcomes and see the activities of teachers and pupils as the means. In other words, I have left open such possibilities as a planner who sets up outcome X, and decides that the best means to reach it is to tell the teacher to aim at Y whilst he tells the pupil he is aiming at Z. Or again, the outcome X might best be achieved incidentally and unconsciously whilst teacher and pupil consciously set out to achieve outcome Y. Though theoretically the rationale I have outlined specifies nothing in itself about the intentions of the participants, it seems to me the nature of the outcomes we are interested in most certainly will. As far as I am aware, for instance, there is no way in which pupils can acquire perceptual concepts without attending to perceptual differences. Again, how can they learn to write or calculate without consciously and deliberately acting in certain ways that are directly related to those outcomes? Or again, if pupils are to become autonomous, capable of personal judgments and determining their own patterns of life, it seems almost inconceivable that such an outcome is possible if the pupils are simply manipulated by others. If, too, teachers are to be instrumental in bringing about outcomes of this kind, it is hardly likely that they could be, let alone would be, prepared to be treated as so many Zombies.

Nevertheless, it must be recognized that many curriculum outcomes are the unconscious products of teacher and pupil activities. And though it is important that curriculum planners are aware of these outcomes and can take them into account in curriculum planning, it is not *obvious* that it is always desirable that the teachers concerned be aware of these outcomes, let alone that the pupils be aware of them as ends. The hidden, unintended curriculum may be in some respects as important as the intended, and that being so, it needs to be enquired into so that it may be brought under control. That is not to say that its outcomes necessarily become the conscious aims of teachers, only that they become the conscious aims of planners.

The possibility of leaving teachers in the dark about what exactly is going on may sound offensive on moral and professional grounds; indeed I think in general it is. For many reasons the choice of curriculum outcomes ought at least in part to be a matter for decision by teachers and not just by planners – whoever they may be. Certainly the case for making decisions about curriculum activities themselves the responsibility of teachers seems very strong indeed. Is not this, after all, the heart of their professional expertise? If it is, then it is imperative that teachers, as well as planners, be aware of the nature of the judgments they make. Rational decisions about the activities are again logically complex practical judgments that necessarily call on many relevant philosophical, psychological, technical, moral and other considerations. What one is compelled to wonder is whether indeed teachers are up to this job. Maybe with aid from experts in the relevant specialisms they are. At present, it is only too true that any systematic justification for what is undertaken by way of curriculum means, is seldom available in the major funded projects. By this I am referring to the justification for the content that is decided on, the methods of teaching or types of learning experiences planned, and the overall programme organization. I am aware that many projects are experimental in character and not attempts to set out a rationally defensible curriculum. Nevertheless, I would have thought that experiment would have best been conducted in terms of both objectives and means that are as defensible as possible. If they are so defensible, then one could expect projects to give that defence.

Everything I have had to say, adds up to a general characterization of curriculum planning as demanding a set of defensible outcomes or ends, for which we plan a defensible programme of means. Because of the nature of the ends, their choice must be based on a wide knowledge of the possibilities, on much philosophical, psychological, sociological knowledge; it involves value judgments of considerable significance. The means, too, can only be responsibly chosen on the basis of a similar range of considerations. But, if here one stops to think what thoroughly rational planning must involve, so overwhelming is the prospect that it is tempting to say that it is impossible. Is not the idea of this approach only acceptable to someone suffering from acute megalomania, someone intoxicated by rationalism run riot? Is there not a paradox one must face, that trying to be thoroughly rational would be completely unreasonable? There is a great deal of truth in this. Let us grant for the sake of the argument, that planning in these terms would be rational if it could be done. But might not the attempt to be rational in certain circumstances be quite irrational nevertheless? Must one not be rational when being rational is appropriate? I think so. Or at least one must recognize the limits of the application of reason in any given context. Rational planning for curriculum outcomes is what it is, and there is no question of evading its demands if we are to do the job rationally. But the actual context in which we have to plan may, for many reasons, permit only limited application of the logical principles involved.

This particular problem has been the burden of a number of philosophers concerned about practical and social planning in general, for instance Karl Popper and Michael Oakeshott (Oakeshott 1962, 1967). A number of curriculum theorists, and in particular J. J. Schwab (Schwab 1969), have examined the problem in the curriculum context. To begin at the most practical level, it is surely a fact that we simply cannot adequately set out the total range of outcomes for a whole school curriculum, if only because we have no satisfactory way of mapping them and their inter-relations. What is more, we could not begin to agree on any proposed set of outcomes at this level. Certainly our gross ignorance of many relevant matters means that we could give no adequate justification for choosing one set rather than another. When it comes to the means, our ignorance on a huge scale re-asserts itself. We simply do not know how to predict many of the outcomes of our actions. Our control over the situation is often amazingly small. But even if we simply do not at present have the knowledge to plan in this total fashion, seeking to select from all the possible ends and using perfectly controlled means, the trouble may be yet more deep-seated, in that yet more psychological or philosophical knowledge would not do the trick for us. When all is said and done, every form of theoretical study is concerned with only one abstract perspective of practical situations. It sees these through one set of concepts. Even within one such relevant study, say psychology, there are fundamental disagreements on learning, motivation or personality development, and these disagreements suggest conflicting practices.

But even if each theoretical approach were not internally coherent, is there any reason to think that we could satisfactorily combine the contributions to our understanding of these fundamentally different approaches? Certainly the idea of a meta-theory uniting the social and other sciences, let alone all the other considerations, seems pretty meaningless. And in any case, why should we assume that the theoretical systems we have at present even begin to exhaust what there is to know, so that we can rationally plan what to do? Maybe it would be wise then to proceed cautiously, making modest modifications in our ends and our means where there seems good reason to change, and where we can keep some control over the situation by preventing the unexpected from overtaking us on a large scale. Let us proceed then from the given situation, planning piecemeal developments, watching carefully the results just because we cannot begin to predict them all. Let us build up slowly, using all the theory there is to help us, a body of knowledge as to what happens on the spot when new things are tried. We must not work on too large a scale, as we will find we cannot then discern clearly precisely why what happened did happen. Let us work by modifying, within limitations, what we have got, and obtaining, by informed trial and error, a progressively extending practical control. Rational planning, as I have tried to outline it, is, if you like, an ideal, whose application necessitates conditions that cannot ever be completely fulfilled. All we can say is that the smaller the scale of planning, and the fewer the variables involved, the more likely we are to succeed. In these circumstances, every attempt at planned curriculum change must be seen as an experient whose outcomes, unintended as well as planned, are in need of assessment and explanation.

Similar points to those I have been trying to make have been expressed by Michael Oakeshott. To him every art, science or practical activity requires for its proper conduct two sorts of knowledge – the technical and the traditional or practical. There is a mass of technical knowledge and information, that can be amassed before an activity is embarked on, and we can try to rationally plan what to do as if this information and the rules that come from it were all that matters. Unfortunately, this approach necessarily ignores all the particular circumstantial complexities of every practical situation. We cannot, for instance, know in advance all the preconceptions and attitudes a particular set of teachers will bring to work with a group of pupils who are likewise unique in their characteristics, in a school with its own individual ethos and traditions. And even if we did know all this theory, it would be merely theory which has somehow to be applied in practical actions. In Oakeshott's view, rational curriculum development can only come about from within traditional or practical knowledge of the business. From this base, in this context alone, modifications can be made using relevant theoretical knowledge so as to make practice more consistent, more effective, etc. Only in this way can one hope to apply successfully what one knows in abstract theoretical terms. Practical knowledge, he insists, is necessary to any development of rational practice. Prior rational planning, imposed on situations without sensitive regard to the unique particulars of the position, must necessarily prove abortive.

Just how, in greater detail, rational development properly takes place, is not easy to discern in Oakeshott's writing, and things are not helped by his view of reason that derives from philosophical idealism. To my mind, rational development in the curriculum can only mean change which conforms to the means-ends considerations I see implicit in a curriculum. There is nothing else it can mean. But accepting Oakeshott's central contention, these considerations must be applied from within existing curriculum practices. Our theoretical knowledge and general principles should be used to make our present activities progressively more reasonable, sensitivity to the particularities of the context being essential. We must also never forget that the most sensitive judgment as to what to do in this situation will result in unexpected, and perhaps undesirable, consequences.

Such a view is indeed to cut rationalism down to size. It is to enjoin on curriculum developers the utmost involvement in current schools practices. And if on other grounds teacher participation in planning does not always seem essential, there are surely here imperative reasons why they should indeed make the judgments about change in the curricula they are involved in, using all that is known of the theoretical considerations. After all, the teachers alone can have the knowledge of the particular context that is involved. But this is not to soften up at all the need for all such developments to be rational in character, the shift in ends and means being justified as far as possible. In this job we have to bring together

24

the contribution of philosophers, psychologists, sociologists and all relevant academic specialists, with that of the teachers. To allow, say, a group of university mathematicians to lay out the objectives of a mathematics course, with concern for no other considerations than those they can bring to the business, to then ask psychologists and sociologists to provide the means, and finally to impose the result on a group of teachers, is indeed rationalism run riot. In the interests of a higher rationality, teachers and pupils have their own ways of coping with such situations, thank goodness. The idea that a philosopher should produce Farmington's moral man and social scientists tell us how to mass produce him, is equally to be dismissed out of court. Any attempt to structure a curriculum on a philosophical analysis of 'forms of knowledge' should be dealt with likewise. We shall get nowhere with such rationalist approaches for they will defeat their own ends. But none of this is to belittle the need for us to accept the partial contribution of mathematicians and philosophers to decisions about curriculum ends or their and other specialists' contributions to judgments about means. It is to insist only that we must start from a detailed knowledge of current practice and, working with those who alone know that practice in Oakeshott's 'traditional' sense, formulate more rational ends and procedures in the light of what relevant theory and experimental evidence there is. The theory alone is not sufficient to develop rational curricula, but neither is ill-considered modification of teachers' practices based on their suggestions alone. It is not good enough for developers to genuflect to philosophers, psychologists and sociologists before proceeding to ignore the important theoretical contributions they have to offer.

Only if we can produce schemes that (a) are based on a thorough grasp of what is actually going on in schools, using all the theory we can to sort that out, (b) proceed to modifications as justifiable as we can make them, and (c) then assess the outcomes intended and unintended, so as to enable us to further understand what is happening, can we really make progress. Our efforts are at present too random. Much we do, no doubt, produces results of interest, and contributes to our practical and theoretical knowledge in a haphazard way. But I am far from certain that our curricula are becoming significantly more rational.

But then is it clear that we know what a rational curriculum would be? That is where I came in. I can only hope my attempts at clarification will contribute something to sorting out our ideas on that question. I certainly believe a little more self-conscious concern about what curriculum development is trying to achieve would do much to direct the limited resources available to us into more profitable channels.

References

EISNER, E. W. (1969) Instructional and Expressive Educational Objectives *AERA Monograph No. 3* Chicago: Rand McNally

GAGNE, R. M. (1965) *The Conditions of Learning* Chs. 8 and 9 New York: Holt, Rinehart and Winston

MCPHAIL, P. (1972) *Moral Education in the Secondary School* London: Longman

OAKESHOTT, M. (1962) *Rationalism in Politics* London: Methuen

OAKESHOTT, M. (1957) Learning and Teaching in *The Concept of Education* (Peters, R. S., ed) London: Routledge

POPPER, K. R. (1945) *The Open Society and Its Enemies* Vol 1. Ch. 19, Vol II. Chs. 17, 24 London: Routledge

SCHWAB, J. J. (1969) The Practical: A Language for Curriculum *School Review* Vol 78 no. 1

STENHOUSE, L. (1970) Some Limitations of the Use of Objectives in Curriculum Research and Planning *Paedagogica Europaea Vol 6*

TYLER, R. W. (1949) *Basic Principles of Curriculum and Instruction* Chicago: University of Chicago Press

The Curriculum for a World of Change

FRANK MUSGROVE
Sarah Fielden Professor of Education,
University of Manchester

I am going to talk about two connected things – postindustrialism and 'the alternative society'. And I shall examine the 'alternative scene' as a kind of curriculum which points to the future.

Economists like Daniel Bell (1967) talk about the post-industrial society; psychologists following Kohlberg talk about a post-conventional morality (Keniston 1969). This is where we're at in education – with a post-industrial society and a post-conventional morality. The post-conventional morality is concerned above all with authenticity and sincerity. But it also questions the unquestionable – like the moral obligation to work, and even the sanctity of the social contract. Like E. M. Forster, it would concede at most two cheers for democracy – and not even that at the cost of an authentic personal relationship. E. M. Forster, like all his Bloomsbury friends – notably Lytton Strachey, Virginia Woolf and Clive Bell – was very 'alternative' indeed. Clive Bell's essay on 'Civilization', written in the 1920s, is still – for all its élitism (or perhaps because of it) – the best blue-print that we have for the curriculum of tomorrow.

But first a few words about change. The experts tell us that its rate and magnitude are without precedent. We are unique in our loss of the stable state. They use easily quantifiable data which computers can handle; extrapolations are made; and the dubious science of futurology is born. We all think we know what an exponential rate of growth looks like. We are all futurologists now.

In fact, in many ways, our rate of social change is uniquely low. The turnover in human beings is very much less than it was a century or two ago. Any given input of human beings can be expected to last for 75 years. In 1750, the expectation of life at birth was 25 years. The rate of change has been reduced by a factor of three.

I think, too, it would be difficult to overstate the retarding effect of secure careers. Not only does nobody die, but nobody gets sacked. Career safeguards are the great bureaucratic invention of the last century. You can't easily sack, or even redeploy, a superfluous

27

department of theologians – or even educationists. You can only wait 30 years for them to retire. We have invented, in comparatively recent years, a very powerful brake on social change. It is certainly holding up the development of automation. It really is folly to produce great armies of second-rate engineers who will spend the next 40 years resisting the computers which would make them redundant.

The stable state was far more precarious when it rested on the family than it is today. When almost any business or enterprise was a family affair, it simply collapsed when the head of the family died, if the sons were still young. And usually they were. On average, in the 17th century, the father died before his eldest son reached maturity. The Companies Act of 1862 made companies immortal. Only men died, and this had now become an irrelevance.

Of course, bureaucratic succession can be used quite deliberately to engineer change. New headmasters are now appointed precisely because they seem likely to undo everything the last man had achieved. This is known as innovation. But it is not a structural necessity. I don't think we need elaborate sociological explanations of contemporary educational innovation. It's really very simple. It's what you get promoted for – and the way you demonstrate that you were worth your promotion.

Nevertheless, there are important ways in which society will change in the next half-century. But I don't think they're crucially different from great social and economic transformations that have occurred previously in Western society. We are constantly losing the stable state, and the consequences are rather boringly similar. Only Americans like Toffler (Toffler 1970) and Schon (Schon 1971), totally devoid of any sense of history, can make extravagant claims for our uniqueness. Toffler, of course, thinks we shall all be in a state of chronic 'future shock'. His only evidence seems to be the curious medical histories of a ship's company in the American Navy during maneuvres in the Pacific. Great theories have been based on less; and some of them are even true. But I should like more compelling evidence.

Something happened in the 1960s. Marcuse called it a 'transvaluation of values' (1969); Adam Curle even talks about 'a new psychic mutation' (1972). Actually, the first generation of a post-industrial society was coming of age – an age of affluence and of openness. The new men are often rebels, not because of their privations, but because of their privileges.

John Barker, Hilary Creek, Anna Mendelson and James Greenfield are now in prison for ten years. They are the extreme case. They are all under 25; they were dropouts from Cambridge and Essex; they

28

were members of the Amherst Road Commune; they were in the Angry Brigade. They had been inspired by the insurrection of May–June, 1968 at the Sorbonne and Nanterre. This was not a cause but a catalyst. Herbert Marcuse was also inspired. He celebrated the events of May–June, in his 'Essay on Liberation', as the harbinger of a new order.

A new man was emerging; the aesthetic principle was replacing the performance principle. 'Today's rebels,' said Marcuse, 'want to see, hear and feel things in a new way: they link liberation with the dissolution of ordinary and orderly perception.' Marcuse, as usual, has got to the very heart of the matter.

Toffler talks about 'future shock', everyone talks about alienation and anomie. I would talk, as Marcuse does, in effect, about openness, which I believe is the central value of our time. This value leads to the rejection of boundaries – emotional, curricular, intellectual, and perceptual-experiential. It underlies apparently diverse phenomena: encounter groups, LSD, community schools, the integrated day. Schools are open-plan, curricula and age groups are integrated, single-honours degrees have become immoral, intellectual activities and examinations are open-ended. These are not descriptions: they are moral imperatives. Openness is the overriding value. And openness is, in the classical Durkheimian sense, anomic.

We are not, in fact, a 'mass society', tightly bonded, over-conforming. We are diverse and deviant. 'The alternative' has a specialized social connotation. Even bureaucracies are 'dynamic', their rules under constant revision – fluid, unpredictable. The nine o'clock news has become a movable feast. Schon sees the loose network, without a firm centre, as the type of modern organization; Toffler talks about 'adhocracy'. Everywhere there are subsects and splinter groups. When the social structure is highly differentiated, as ours is, it would be remarkable if the culture were not correspondingly diverse.

The boundaries are coming down. The 'alternative' – whether the Free School or the commune – points roughly, I believe, to the future. The challenge of the next decade is to create a society fit for outsiders to live in. The challenge for the curriculum is to offer some preparation for a life which must be ever less linear, increasingly episodic and open-ended.

I have been interviewing people in the 'alternative' – in communes, mystical sects, anarchist groups, Free Schools, Rank-and-File, Rebel, and the National Union of School Students. Of course, they are not all equally 'alternative': the NUSS is almost as establishment as the TUC. I always ask them how they got in. (I am interested in the alternative as a social process: the steps and incidents, the career, as it were, which lead to outsider or counter positions.) People in all these alternative spheres invariably refer to being – or having been – 'loners'. Their sense of social attachment is very weak. They do not seem to have what Adam Curle has recently called a strong 'belonging-identity'. And because they have a very weak 'belonging-identity', they would meet with Adam Curle's approval.

Adam Curle has a very undersocialized conception of man. In his recent book, *Mystics and Militants*, he distinguishes between awareness-identity and belonging-identity. Awareness-identity is not anchored in social relationships; it is found, he thinks, among people who have adopted (whether full-time or part-time) so-called alternative life-styles. It is the distinguishing characteristic of mystics and those who have joined communes.

My own work gives some support to this view. Thus a prominent 17-year-old leader of the NUSS said in the course of a long, semi-structured interview: 'Since childhood, I've always had long periods of isolation. I was very much a recluse sometimes. I've never felt part of things. My childhood was rather confused, and I never felt I could express myself properly.' A 27-year-old university dropout, now a full-time mystic, said: 'We regard Tibetan Buddhism very highly, but we tend away from most *Hindu* things because they are concerned with morality. We have no society. We are outside society.'

I have a good deal of evidence, from work with a wide range of people from 16 to 60, that anyone of any age who strongly supports boundary-bursting 'alternative' or counter-cultural values seldom defines himself in social terms. Adam Curle would applaud this; I think he underrates the problems raised. He wants us all to develop awareness-identity and be done with belonging. (Actually, we shall probably have no option.) Work that I have been doing shows three closely related circumstances among those who have accepted 'alternative' values: high scores on a scale of counter-cultural values, high scores on a scale of anomie, and subconsensual self-concepts. Low scorers, on the contrary, appear not to be anomic, and they answer the existential question *Who Are You?* in terms of their social relationships and statuses – like the 45-year-old woman who said: 'Well, I'm the daughter of a retired professor, the sister of a colonel and the cousin of a brigadier. I'm the wife of an engineer, the mother of a banker, I belong to a right-wing political party, and I'm a tall Nordic type.' (She was a very low scorer indeed on my counter-cultural scale – almost as low as the daughter of a 'fine Southern gentleman' in one of my American samples.)

Now I would not see the non-social self-concept as the sign of a new psychic mutation: its roots lie in the social dislocation that arises from rapid social change. But I would not equate rapid change with inventions and their diffusion. The really crucial circumstance is population growth, movement, and concentration in large urban and suburban centres. So it was at the time of the Reformation and the birth of capitalism: the Puritan Ethic was a search for a new interactional norm during the build-up of great commercial cities. The roots of the 'alternative' are demographic.

The problem is to find a sense of identity in a world of circumstance. The counter-culture is a sort of curriculum which young people are inventing to explore shifting realities and discover a sense of personal meaning. Often it goes sour. Or just becomes a bore. It is difficult to remain exquisitely expressive and non-instrumental for years on end. There is already a sense that the 1960s were a 'bad trip'. Adam Curle, Charles Reich (1971) and Roszak (1970) have romanticized the counter-culture. For its current authentic voice, read Oz – notably the February 1973 number which contains John Hoyland's brilliantly perceptive article, 'The Long March Through the Bingo Halls'. At the heart of the counter-culture there is disorder. But it is disorder we have to learn to live with.

The counter-culture is aesthetic-expressive rather than pragmatic-instrumental, intuitive rather than rational. And it is non-deferential – against power, especially bureaucratic power. 'Ring your own Bloody Bell' – as R. G. Gregory, Head of Drama at Market Drayton Comprehensive School, said to the headmaster during a series of remarkable encounters in 1971 (Gregory 1971).

In the counter-culture there is not only a distaste for other people's authority, but for exercising it oneself. Increasingly people – and not least beginning teachers – will refuse jobs which, they feel, 'force them to be bastards'. Young teachers I've talked to in Free Schools gave up teaching jobs and went on the dole, because they didn't want a job in which they'd got to be 'something of a bastard' over the next 40 years. Meetings of Rank-and-File express this same concern. Teaching precludes being civilized – certainly as Clive Bell conceived civilization. You will recall his dictum: 'The mere exercise of power, the coercing of others, will tinge a man with barbarism' (Bell 1938). My NUSS interviewees are profoundly sorry for teachers who, they say, are forced to be bastards by the system. Which is a pity, because they're nice chaps, really.

The counter-culture is Dionysiac, not Apollonian: heady, intoxicated, tactile, erotic. It is the other face of order: the frenzied corn-god at the heart of systematic Neolithic agriculture; self-flagellants in 13th-century Siena, just when they were inventing double-entry book-keeping; the high point of witchcraft in 16th-century England, just when Puritan rationality was promoting modern capitalism and science. And it is also, as Nietzsche said in *The Birth of Tragedy*, the music of Wagner : Valhalla and Valkyries. But Apollonian man is the potter-painter-sculptor : he imposes himself on nature, moulds it and shapes it, gives boundaries to shapes. He is thus an author, and so has authority. He is competent, well-organized, a good statistician. He is the law-maker-engineer. He has been fashioned most perfectly over the past two centuries in the French Grandes Écoles. He is a graduate of the École Normale Supérieure. And he is obsolescent.

Nietzsche foresaw it all. Dionysus is at one with nature; and, like the hippies' flowers hung on Russian tanks during the invasion of Prague, his chariot is bedecked with flowers and garlands : 'panthers and tigers pass beneath its yoke.' 'Believe with me,' said Nietzsche, 'in Dionysian life and the re-birth of tragedy. The time of Socratric man is past : crown yourselves with ivy, take in your hands the thyrsus, and do not marvel if tigers and panthers lie down fawning at your feet' (Nietzsche 1909).

There is a curious interaction, interdependence or dialectic between the Apollonian and the Dionysian. It reaches a level of unusual intensity at times of economic transformation. This inter-dependence is found at the ideological and at the personal levels. Shelley is incongruously but inextricably linked with Thomas Love Peacock, Coleridge with Dr Gillman, Swinburne with Watts-Dunton, Francis Thompson with the Meynells. This is not neces-sarily a parasitic relationship. But the outsider position can be deeply disturbing. Shelley once lost his nerve and asked Peacock to get him a job in the India Office. Coleridge actually became secretary to the Governor of Malta. Middle-aged hippies become Directors-General of the BBC.

And now for the counter-culture as curriculum – exploratory in character, like all the best curricula, often taking roads which are cul-de-sacs or worse, but searching for personal meaning. It is a very open curriculum – and it has less coherence than I am suggesting. Its main ingredient is travel, especially Eastern travel. The really vital piece of curricular equipment is a sleeping-bag.

Of course it is a strictly nonvocational curriculum : indeed, it is against work in any traditional sense, and it deeply rejects the Protestant work ethic. As one of our activist-anarchist interviewees said – he's a university graduate living on Social Security – 'I tried work once, for about six months. It was all right. But work fucks your mind.' How right he is. William Godwin, in his 'Inquiry Concerning Political Justice', didn't say it better.

Another of our interviewees, a 30-year-old activist, ended a long interview by saying, 'Young people and students should get more experience. I don't think they should *work* – don't get me wrong. They should just put on a knapsack and bum off round the world. That's what I would like my kids to do. I don't suppose they will because I want them to.' He is an interesting man who was formerly a farm labourer and spent various periods in prison for civil disobedience. He is now a mature university student in the third year of an honours degree in Anthropology. His current mode of dropping out is to drop in. This also, I think, points to the university of the future. It also shows how educational curricula and institutions can change their meaning while retaining their structure and rhetoric. The university, unnoticed, becomes a place where dropouts drop in.

The 'alternative scene' as a curriculum consists of experiences, exposures and experiments: a milieu, rather than a structure, for personal discovery, growth and development. It is not, of course, a perfect model, ready-made for widespread adoption in schools. But this, I suggest, is where one must look for some insight into a meaningful curriculum for the future.

Any social system is a core of stable beliefs and values surrounded by a margin of experimental and disreputable practices. Our attention should be turned to the margin. We should understand the process which selects disreputable practices, makes them legitimate, and incorporates them in the stable core. How are they legitimized? Do they have to be sanctified by HMIs, the Schools Council, particularly prestigeful headmasters? Most so-called innovation is in fact the *diffusion* of legitimized and already routine and rather tired practices. Often it is already thoroughly emasculated. Can we legitimize the disreputable most easily for diffusion in the low-status areas of education?

This counter-cultural curriculum arises largely from the participants' prior values; but it is also a problem-solving curriculum for dealing with pressing problems of sheer survival. It calls for far more ingenuity and resourcefulness than the Outward Bound. In this respect it is astonishingly like the curriculum that William Cobbett invented on his farm to educate his sons. It has a strong legal element. Cobbett had to understand the intricacies of the Poor Law; in 'the alternative' you have to know about the laws of trespass, and above all the laws surrounding social security. And you need to know something about plumbing and baking bread.

In the cognitive domain, the main elements are these: extensive biological-physiological knowledge, especially for its bearing on foodstuffs, additives, impurities, vegetarianism, and drug use; chemical-geographical knowledge, especially with regard to the

33

C

environment and pollution; psychological knowledge (the counter-culture solidly supports 'People Not Psychiatry'): political philosophy – not only Marx and Marcuse, but the 17th-century Diggers and Levellers; Eastern Philosophy and Comparative Religion; Anthropology; and, of course, Astrology.

Its 'set books', as it were, are principally science-fiction; but include A. S. Neill, Norman Cohn and R. D. Laing (1957), Blake and the *Prelude*. (For some whom we've interviewed the set books are ancient Egyptian texts which they themselves are translating. Their knowledge of hieroglyphics is awe-inspiring.) It is a curriculum remarkable for information-storage and information-processing, in relation to travel, 'crash-pads', and legal aid. But in the 'affective domain' we have bead-work, leather-work, poetry, music, chanting, contemplation, tactile communication, body-movements and postures. And the values it promotes are compassion, sincerity, sharing, self-denial, frugality, joy and spontaneity, and tolerance of dirt. At its heart is a tolerance of disorder – just as Edmund Leach, the Provost of King's, in a famous counter-cultural manifesto, apparently would wish.

Boundary-removal and the rejection of hierarchy come together in tactile experience – in encounter groups. The counter-culture is essentially inclusive. Academic hierarchies are stroked to extinction. No headmaster can ever bestride the platform again after he's been stroked by the girls of the Lower Sixth.

We have serious theoretical problems in trying analysis at the micro-level – through our highly personal interview material – to macro-level analysis. The meaning that actors see is not necessarily the meaning of the action. Perhaps this should not detain us, but it has wider implications for the study of curricula.

Curriculum development today is largely senseless, because of the disjunction between micro-level and macro-level analysis. Different explanatory models are used at the two levels, and there is no necessary connection between them. At the micro-level it is all individual motives, aims, objectives; at the macro-level we have social functions, and the two seem to vary, independently. This is analogous to the disjunction between the meaning and the structure of institutions – analytically distinct components which don't necessarily explain each other. Are organized games a substitute for sodomy; the basis of national character; a legalistic training in rule understanding, observation and enforcement: a deepening of aesthetic sensibilities through the symmetry and contours of a game of football? The same structure can have any of these meanings. And often institutional rhetoric hides the truth. There is a dissociation

34

between structure and meaning which curriculum developers should ponder.

The function of the counter-culture at the macro-level has to be seen in terms of the nature and needs of a post-industrial economy. And this economy really has the problem of wealth-production solved. The difficult problems are those of distribution. Work in industrial production, at all levels, shrinks. Generally there is less work; but the personal-service professions grow.

Curiously, it is personal-service activities in which the counter-culture is heavily engaged. This bothers them, because they feel that instead of being genuinely alternative they are merely giving 'social aspirins' which prevent the revolution. They live off social security but do the Social Security's work for it – in helping gypsies, exploited and dispossessed tenants, drug addicts, the homeless and the mentally ill. They are constantly arguing whether they should be freaks working only for freaks. But essentially I would say they are really putting a nonvocational curriculum to the final test. Work has traditionally done two things for us – at the personal level it has given our lives meaning, and at the level of society it has bound us together. Even the division of labour, as Durkheim saw, does not divide man from man, but promotes interdependence and social cohesion. At both levels we're going to have a problem. The counter-culture tentatively explores possible solutions.

The counter-culture is the pervasive spirit of a new generation. Functionalists like Eisenstadt (1956), and Ellul in his book, *The Techological Society* (1965), have to argue that new generational values are not the agents or symptoms of change, but are essentially adaptive, integrative, supportive of the status quo. They are trapped in the characteristic circularity of functionalist analysis. I am sure that something very important and new – though not without parallels – is happening. We have a new spirit of the age in the sense in which Ortega y Gasset used that term : with a generational base which is the pivot of history (Ortega y Gasset 1931).

The 'function' of a generation can be interpreted as the selection and re-interpretation of knowledge. Ortega y Gasset argued that some generations refuse this historical mission – refuse to be the pivots of history. But generally, they take it on. Generational selection of knowledge is made in the light of the particular historical consciousness which really constitutes a generation – the product of particular historical experiences. We as teachers may reject a generation's 'selection' of knowledge. But I think we ignore it at our peril. Every generation must write its own history and literary criticism. Of course this is done by a highly sophisticated

35

minority. But the minority simply brings into focus the stirrings of an entire generation.

We can only behave sensibly in educational planning and curriculum development if we take this generational consciousness into account – not only for the clues afforded by its content, but for its loose and shifting organizational framework. Clearly much education at the secondary stage must be taken out of schools. It makes sense in terms of a changing economy and social structure : essentially it is anticipating the displacement of work from the centrality it has enjoyed in our lives since Luther brought it out of the monastery and sanctified it for profit. It is tackling the problem of human significance and worth without work.

The Romantics made an abortive attempt to do this nearly 200 years ago. They were very aware of rapid change : they knew even then that knowledge decays exponentially, that curricula are piled high with decay, and that schoolboys emerge with a lingering smell of death. Godwin in particular attacked the dysfunctional permanence of curricula, and on these grounds became the first de-schooler.

They were against work and careers; they favoured episodic rather than linear (Apollonian) life-styles – their lives by our standards were disorderly, picaresque; and they stood four-square for joy. Even Bentham took 'happiness' as his criterion for legislation and was sternly rebuked by Carlyle for his levity. Keats was all for pleasure which was sensationalist, psychedelic, direct and voluptuous. The fun ethic is not the invention of today's generation. It is not a twentieth century discovery of Martha Wolfenstein (1951).

In the 'Preface' to the *Lyrical Ballads*, Wordsworth claimed that poetry was 'a homage paid to the native and naked dignity of man, to the grand elementary principle of pleasure . . . .' And that is what it is still all about – human worth and dignity in circumstances of technological advance and bureaucratic constraint which seem to deny their possibility. Today Marcuse talks about it in a more Freudian idiom – in terms of the eroticization of the personality. We must all explore hitherto unsuspected, but nonetheless exquisite, erogenous zones. Our cybernetic revolution in the production of wealth finally makes all this possible. It provides the structure for the new culture. But just how it does so is another lecture.

Note: The interviews reported in this paper were made possible by a grant from the SSRC for research into counter-cultural associations.

References

BELL, CLIVE (1938) *Civilization* London : Penguin Books

BELL, DANIEL (1967) *Daedalus* Summer issue

COHN, N. (1957) *The Pursuit of the Millenium* London : Secker and Warburg

CURLE, A. (1972) *Mystics and Militants* London : Tavistock

EISENSTADT, S. N. (1956) *From Generation to Generation* London : Routledge

ELLUL, JACQUES (1965) *The Technological Society* (trans. J. Wilkinson) London : Jonathan Cape

GASSET, J. ORTEGA Y. (1931) *The Modern Theme* (trans. J. Cleugh) Daniel Company

GREGORY, R. G. (1971) *The Grove* (duplicated : Wrekin Libertarians)

LAING, R. D. (1965) *The Divided Self* Harmondsworth : Penguin

MARCUSE, H. (1969) *An Essay on Liberation* Allen Lane, The Penguin Press

NIETZSCHE, FREDRICH (1909) *The Birth of Tragedy* (trans W. A. Haussmann) London : Foulis

REICH, C. A. (1971) *The Greening of America* Allen Lane, The Penguin Press

ROSZAK, T. (1970) *The Making of a Counter Culture* London : Faber

SCHON, D. A. (1971) *Beyond the Stable State* London : Temple Smith

SLATER, P. E. (1970) *The Pursuit of Loneliness* Boston : Beacon Press

TOFFLER, A. (1970) *Future Shock* London : Bodley Head

WOLFENSTEIN, MARTHA (1951) The Emergence of Fun Morality *Journal of Social Issues*

Section 1: Practical Curriculum Development

Introduction

W. G. ALLAN RUDD
University of Manchester

This section reviewed experience of curriculum development work accumulated in national, local and within-school settings during the past five years. Section membership included teachers, head-teachers, teachers' centre leaders, LEA advisers and administrators, workers from national development projects, university and college of education lecturers and visitors from Sweden and the USA. Papers were presented by Professor Alan Blyth, Director, Schools Council Project, *History, Geography and Social Sciences 8–13*, and by Dr Allan Rudd, Director, *North West Regional Curriculum Development Project*.

Between these presentations the section considered case studies and examples of problems and successes in practical curriculum development, drawing largely on members' own experiences. First, the headmaster of an open-plan primary school outlined a scheme in which a group of neighbouring schools facing similar curriculum problems are to work together in developing resource materials and teaching units. After another member had outlined a similar scheme under way in another part of the country in relation to the problems of teaching immigrant children, the section discussed the isolation felt by many teachers in their own classrooms, and the value of pooling ideas for dealing with common problems.

Next, the head of a reading centre outlined the transition in his work during the past decade from emphasis upon a remedial service for children to inservice work for teachers of reading. The inservice courses, which had been running since 1969, stress an understanding of the process of reading development; knowledge of appropriate methods and media for teaching reading; methods of identifying and treating individual children who have special difficulties; psychological and sociological aspects of reading and reading difficulties; and organization of the teaching of reading in the school and classroom. This outline eventually led to general agreement that, though teachers could gain much mutual enlightenment and support from the pooling of their ideas, there was also need for input of information and other ideas from specialist sources, academic and professional.

This recognition led a teachers' centre leader to reflect on the conception of a teachers' centre. Whilst recognizing that such centres had, during the past five years, provided many support services for schools these services were largely of two types: making available resource materials which schools might need but could not afford individually, and providing short inservice courses led by LEA advisers or other authoritative persons. He claimed that neither of these services was the *main* purpose for which teachers' centres had been established; and he went on to list six conditions which ought to be met if teacher-led curriculum development were to be undertaken productively in such centres. This led to a brief discussion on the relative merits of specialist-led and autonomous-teacher-led schemes of curriculum development in local settings, and later to contrasts between centralized and decentralized organizations for development work. The section's Swedish visitor then briefly reported on a development scheme currently under way in a sparsely-populated area of his country, in which curricula suitable for use in non-streamed classes in all-age schools were being worked out. He claimed that national and local agencies had to combine effectively in this project; for if they failed, the children concerned would have to leave home for their education, and rural depopulation would probably follow.

The section then moved on to discussing the creative role which a liberal LEA administration might play in supporting curriculum reform in local contexts. Examples were given of ways in which subtle but very effective constraints upon teacher initiative could be exercised by an insensitive administration when rules for teacher representation on the local centre management committee or principles of financing local development work were being drawn up.

Finally, a researcher studying the rate of diffusion and the geographical distribution of schools adopting Nuffield O Level courses in the three sciences presented data which showed:

(a) that to date the rate of uptake of these courses in this country was not dissimilar to that found in respect of comparable innovations in the USA and elsewhere.

(b) that the schools where trials had been held during the developmental stage seem to be acting as nuclei during the diffusion stage of Nuffield science projects.

This report reassured section members and also drew attention to the time perspective necessary in planning curriculum reform in a national context.

History, Geography and Social Science 8-13: A Second-generation Project

ALAN BLYTH
University of Liverpool

In presenting this subject to the Conference, I feel uncomfortably like a Prince of Wales or, if you prefer, the heir-apparent to a parliamentary seat. But I am bound to say that the title does epitomize exactly what we are, and what I am profoundly grateful that we are. For it is already clear that the first generation of curriculum development projects was, inevitably, involved in breaking the soil and initiating processes so novel and so wide-ranging that it was virtually inevitable that they would raise almost as many problems as they solved.

It is, perhaps, significant that a project on history, geography and social science *was* a second-generation development. As some of you will know, the Schools Council started off with major initiatives in some fields that required urgent action, such as ROSLA, and also took over other concerns started by the Nuffield Foundation which had been particularly interested in languages, mathematics and science. Ritual gestures of appreciation had been made towards the humanities and social studies, in the middle years, but in general it was assumed that they would be looked after by someone else. Geography was then catered for, in the older adolescent years; Denis Lawton succeeded in getting the Council interested in the development of social-science concepts in the 8–13 years; eventually, history too became a matter for attention.

Following the submission of the Lawton Report (Lawton, Campbell and Burkitt 1971), to whose pioneering work we are greatly indebted, the Council decided to launch a development project not only to remedy the proven deficiency in social science materials for the middle years but also to monitor the contribution of history and geography to the curriculum at that stage and to ensure that materials for this, too, were built up. So, after much negotiation, our project was launched; almost the last project to cover a major curricular area that had been previously neglected. When I, as Director of this Project, first took stock of the position and began to decide what course of action to follow, I at once became well aware of the debt that my future colleagues and I

already owed to our forerunners and in particular to a few significant curriculum development projects in cognate fields. Perhaps I
might indicate the nature of that debt by referring to those projects
one by one, indicating in particular how they affected our thinking,
rather than describing our work more generally in a way that is
available in our *Interim Statement* (Blyth *et al* 1972).

I thought when we started, and I still think, that the two projects
from which we would have most to learn were *Science 5/13* and the
Humanities Project. This was because we were commissioned to
undertake, within a part of the age-band covered by *Science 5/13* an
operation broadly comparable to theirs within a similarly extensive
sector of the accepted middle-years curriculum, but one which
corresponded fairly closely to the subject concerns of the Humanities Project. As you will appreciate, both these projects, together
with some others of direct concern to us, had already acquired a
considerable national reputation and so in spite of the genial readi-
ness with which their Directors and staffs shared ideas with us, we
felt, rather nervously perhaps, that we were in distinguished
company. But their national reputation and their generosity were
among the few features that *Science 5/13* and the Humanities
Project did have in common. For the rest, they indicated neatly just
how divergent the approaches to curriculum development could be,
and how necessary it would be, at the outset, to take stock of
existing developments and to make meaningful choices before planning our own strategy in detail. This, I think, is the distinctive
characteristic of a 'second-generation' project and I think it will be
consonant with the aim of this Section if I spend a little time in
developing this theme.

As you will know, *Science 5/13* is essentially an objectives-based
project. An early development in that project's history was the
formulation of a table of objectives which subsequently developed
into the now familiar booklet *With Objectives in Mind* (Ennever and
Harlen 1969). It is in its way a classic, something of a milestone in
English curriculum development. It was devised in the light of the
Bloom taxonomy, which became quite familiar in this country
during the 1960s, and it represents a very interesting combination
of the taxonomy itself, which appears to postulate a *logical*
sequence in each major 'domain', with the *developmental* emphasis
derived from the Piagetian school which was also prominent during
the past decade. This combination had a considerable pedagogical
justification. According to Piaget and his school, there is a general
development of children's cognitive powers toward higher levels of
abstraction and generalization, as they grow from infancy through
to older adolescence. If this is generally true, (generally, because

there can also be an infinity of sub-cycles related to specific cognitive functions), then it seems reasonable to assert that this cognitive growth enables children to attain, as they pass through the years of school, higher levels in the Bloom taxonomy. And since it is claimed that this *is* a true taxonomy, that is, that adequate attainment of the higher levels depends on prior facility at the lower levels, the model of cognitive development put forward by *Science 5/13* has considerable claims to be capable of offering a general model for the curriculum as a whole.

It is therefore necessary to look closely and critically at its theoretical basis. Scrutiny of the Bloom taxonomy is now a familiar occupation and it is hardly necessary to indicate the reservations that have been expressed about its use. Having been devised in the context of examinations, it has tended to stress the measurable, the rational and the logical rather than the expressive, the open-ended and the holistic aspects of a curriculum. The division of the taxonomy into 'domains', and the palpably greater success of the work on the cognitive when compared with the affective domain, in fact epitomizes some of its limitations. This does not in any way detract from the scale or the importance of the operation which produced the taxonomy; it is simply a caveat about using it too readily in curriculum development.

This is especially true when considering an area of the curriculum which is not necessarily based on logical progression, one concept following another in a relatively necessary order. For *Science 5/13* it served fairly well; probably it would, for mathematics too; for art education it probably would not. For history, geography and social science it seemed to have some validity, but less than for the sciences, and still less than for mathematics. And within any major area it could have the drawback of emphasizing those aspects that were open to point-by-point evaluation, such as the 'lower-level' skill and knowledge objectives, at the expense of those which, though allowed for in the taxonomy at the higher levels, made much more demand on planning and evaluation alike.

As for the other, Piagetian, basis of the *Science 5/13* strategy, it has been developed largely through empirical studies of logical and scientific thinking rather than through the handling of concepts about human behaviour. The applicability of Piaget's ideas on cognitive and moral development to the curriculum in the humanities and social sciences has not been universally accepted, and further specific research in this area is needed (McNaughton 1966).

So, when considering the basic document of the *Science 5/13* project, we had to indicate explicit reservations about its applicability to our concerns. We did, of course, note that the *Science 5/13* team does not prescribe in detail how their framework of objectives should govern the actual teaching within schools; on the contrary, they encourage teachers to choose their own means of implementing the objectives and even to allow the children some say in what objectives they were to pursue. But we also noted that teachers had sometimes tended to look to the framework, and to the materials produced in accordance with it, as a precise guide for action rather than an example of how to proceed. Comparing the subject-matter area involved in *Science 5/13* with our own, we felt, in fact, that we should exercise all the caution that the Science team had shown, more than some of their interpreters had shown, and then rather more than that, since our own subject-matter was so much more difficult to order logically in a sequence, even a major sequence, from 8 to 13.

In making this divergence from an objectives-based approach, we could of course learn substantially from the Humanities Project. For reasons with which everyone here will probably be familiar, the Humanities Project has become better known to the lay public for the outcome of its strategy than for its basis. But the basis is largely responsible for the outcome. Instead of starting from objectives, Lawrence Stenhouse and his team started from content and its significance. Instead of concentrating on output, they emphasized input, though these terms have rather specific meanings. The strategy which they generated, the role of the neutral chairman, the production of large packs within which choice is left strictly indeterminate; all of this is familiar to those who have been initiated into the use of the Humanities approach. What is not always so well remembered is that it is considered to be necessary because of the nature and significance of the content and that considerable emphasis has always been laid on the necessity for enquiry into central human problems, on the co-ordinated contribution of *disciplines* such as English and history to such enquiry, and on the logical structure of those disciplines (Stenhouse 1968–9). It is this that informs the major topics and acts as a filter in respect of choice of materials. This stands in fairly clear contrast to the Science project which, while postulating scientific thinking among its objectives, would not wish to claim that content areas such as chemistry, or geology, as such constitute groups of objectives. For a project required by its terms of reference to consider the specific contributions, but also the interrelations, of history, geography and social science, the thinking and the experience of the Humanities Project was clearly relevant.

Here again, of course, closer scrutiny might suggest that there are implicit objectives even though they are much broader than those derived from the Bloom taxonomy. The roles assigned to teacher and pupil, the nature of the content of packs, even the maintenance of an apparatus of initiation conferences, all indicate that the major objectives of the project itself were in fact very thoroughly thought out, though not in the familiar Bloomian mode. The sort of objectives framework which was central to *Science 5/13* was notably absent from the Humanities Project.

You will appreciate what I mean when I say that we had to make a major choice at the outset. Actually, our terms of reference, for whose formulation I must admit some responsibility, almost obliged us to choose both alternatives. I will quote an extract referring to the production of materials, underlining the points relevant to the present discussion:

> It would be virtually essential to formulate *specific objectives* before (this) material could be purposefully devised, and therefore some attention would inevitably be paid to '*teaching method' in the broadest sense*, examples of what appear to be good current practice, but also, necessarily, *innovations in practice*. Since there is, in spite of the range of individual differences among children, a substantial developmental interval between the ages of 8 and 13, involving also the transition between two, and possibly three, schools, particular attention should be paid to the question of *progression in learning* and especially to the relation between *development in children* and the *specific logical structures of history, geography and social science*.... Blooms taxonomy

So it continues. To the novice, as I then was, it sounded convincing and comprehensive. To Lawrence Stenhouse, who gave me an urgent tutorial on it, it sounded the epitome of self-contradiction. I went away thoughtful; and eventually decided after all rather in favour of *Science 5/13*. The reason was really that the type of indirection which characterized the Humanities Project in action appeared, in crude terms, to make social and emotional demands rather in excess of the capacity of children between 8 and 13.

This was our major decision. We decided to formulate objectives, for teachers to foster among children. But before I take the epic further, I must briefly refer to the other first-generation projects which we also took into account.

It would be appropriate next to mention the North West Curriculum Development Project directed by Dr Allan Rudd, since this is his Section. Actually, we did not find it possible to follow his project very closely. Our own team had been fairly generously staffed with the intention of acting as the focus of innovation; his project, on the other hand, was intended to be based on local teachers' groups and was funded accordingly. But it was clearly possible to draw on the experience of the Manchester project for one central purpose, that of its successful blend of theoretical study of curriculum development with a practical outcome.

A similar consideration applied to our local 'Childwall Development Project', the scheme fostered by the Liverpool LEA to meet ROSLA from which publications have recently emerged. David Wyn Evans, its Director, has developed a series of packs on various themes in conjunction with Liverpool teachers and, although most of these are for school-leavers, at least one is now for the middle years.

Better known nationally, not least for the colourful figure of its Director, is the Liverpool EPA Project. Dr Eric Midwinter had been closely in touch with me for some time before our own project began, and I think that ours is probably the only instance of a Schools Council venture that is second-generation to an EPA venture. To be accurate, we are not working in the same schools as *Priority* (the Liverpool Project's name) since we are trying to spread both the load and, we hope, the benefit for the schools. But Dr Midwinter and I have periodic discussions which are stimulating and necessary, and we are on each other's Committees, which usually means in practice that we exchange apologies! However, our own project will never now be able to forget that schools do have community settings and that these materially influence curriculum.

The nearest project in actual subject-matter terms to our own was Environmental Studies: in fact, it could be regarded as a major contribution within our area, and one that has produced quite significant publications of its own. Melville Harris himself is also on our Consultative Committee and has been most helpful. Indeed, I and my colleagues would have been pleased to have more first-generation project directors on our Committee but protocol did not permit this and Mel Harris got there not as a Project Director but as a Welshman.

There are many other forerunners that could be included but I will mention only one more, the Keele Integrated Studies Project, because our own obligation to consider inter-relation has led a number of people to consider that we, too, are an Integrated Studies Project. The confusion has perhaps been heightened because David Bolam is an historian, and historical material has figured quite prominently in the Keele publications. But in any case there is an interaction between the Keele project and ours at the level of ideas and evaluation and to some extent, since we have some trial schools in South Cheshire, in territory also. There is even one sense in which we are experiencing anew our debt to this particular first-generation project, since we can now observe what happens when a publisher is directly involved with materials bearing some resemblance to our own.

We started, therefore, with a fund of experience and indeed of generosity on which to build. It would be uncharitable of me also to spell out some of the warnings that we received, based as they were on the less fortunate experiences of earlier projects. These, too, we have tried to heed. In order to be quite fair, I will at once admit that we ourselves have a very important practical warning to pass on; but what it is, I will leave till the very end.

When we came to the next step, that of actually planning our own trials, we found it useful to consider our forerunners in another way too. It seems logical to suggest that involvement in sponsored curriculum development is a cumulative experience and that anyone who has actually taken part in, let us say, Primary French, will come to a project like ours with some sort of perception of 'a project' and what it involves and perhaps, also, with some already modified attitudes to what school is for. It would hardly be defensible if the nation were to conduct its procedures collectively in such a way that a school can, as it were, absorb only one project at a time, still less if it can absorb only one altogether. This would scarcely result in a balanced curriculum. At the same time there is a possible danger that working with another project could actually result in undue bias or distortion. So we deliberately elected to involve some schools, under some LEAs, just because they had already had experience of *Science 5/13*, Environmental Studies, the Humanities Project, Nuffield Primary Mathematics or Nuffield Primary French. As a bonus, too, we encountered teachers with previous experience of other projects, and we are watching with some interest to see what effect this prior involvement appears to have. We are not yet in a position to comment with authority on this point; but it will figure in our evaluation.

I should like next to indicate what we have added to the distilled experience of our predecessors, and how we came by these additional features of the project. Every new venture is surely expected to develop some original features and, looking back after eighteen months, I think I can say that our few pieces of originality have all developed as a result of a rather uncomfortable process. First, we felt that previous projects left something out, but we were not quite sure what it was. Next, we drew up memoranda saying what we thought it was. Then we found that all our memoranda were mutually contradictory, so we held a meeting, after which we had become still more contradictory. Soon after, we held a second meeting and began to feel that we were getting a little closer together instead of further apart. Finally, we wrote a further draft and found that we had agreed on something that went beyond our starting-point.

The first venture of this sort was when we decided not merely to draw up objectives, something like *Science 5/13*, but to organize our field work round *key concepts* based on the approach developed by the late Hilda Taba and her colleagues in California. We selected seven: communication, power, values and beliefs, consensus/conflict, similarity/difference, continuity/change and causality. The idea was that these would give some shape to the content used in pursuit of the objectives. We held a national conference for our trial teachers and managed to secure agreement, perhaps with some persuasion from the team, about the objectives and key concepts for use during the trials. In fact, we are spending four crowded terms in 31 schools producing over one hundred 'units' in accordance with the objectives and key concepts and it seems possible, cautiously, to claim that we are conveying to the teachers the purpose of working on these lines.

This brings me directly to our second major innovation. In order to explain this adequately, I should like to go back for a moment to the beginning of the project and mention one rather controversial point that we had in mind from the outset. By 1970 it was beginning to be thought that some, at least, of the development work that had previously been undertaken was proving less permanent in its impact than had been expected. Two main explanations for this were currently being discussed. One was that project teams, and others, were so bound up with the success of projects that it was in nobody's interest to point out their defects. (It is to the honour of the Humanities Project that it always did allow for, and scrutinize, failure). To cater in part for this, we included in our team an evaluator whose task was not just to test the effectiveness of materials for the attainment of limited objectives, but also to stand back and appraise the project itself. It was made clear, when he was appointed, that his own prospects would be in no way worsened if his professional judgment led him to point out weaknesses in the project's outcome.

But there was another possible explanation of the failure of previous projects to make a lasting impact. This was that they had concentrated on a combination of materials and publicity, rather than on the social processes involved in getting curriculum innovations accepted and adapted. In the apt and now familiar phrase which Professor Eric Hoyle has coined, they did not allow for 'tissue rejection' (Hoyle 1969, 1970). Our project gained from its late inception because this danger was already apparent, for example in the field of secondary science, before our plans were fully made. We allocated, from the start, a considerable part of our time and effort to the programme of diffusion that would be necessary. It had been the policy of the Humanities Project to estimate their success in terms not of what happened in their trial schools, but of what transfer effect the trial-school experience exercised elsewhere. This was another way in which the Humanities experience acted as a guide to us. But, in our thinking, it was linked with the one other general feature which I have not yet mentioned, but which is common to most if not all of the projects that were available for us to consider, and which is indeed central to what might be called the ideology of most curriculum development in this country.

This feature is, that each teacher should be free to select, adapt or reject suggestions, materials and procedures according to his or her own professional judgment. Sometimes, I think, this principle has been honoured in name rather than in substance. It is not easy, when confronted with a dazzlingly complete set of materials and handbooks, to regard these as mere instances of what might be done. He would indeed be a bold and dedicated teacher who could realistically expect, in addition to his regular daily obligations, to rival even in a small measure the products of a project manned by an expert full-time team. With our emphasis on diffusion, we set out to avoid this outcome by institutionalizing, from the outset, the context-specific nature of genuine curriculum process. The way (oversimplified) in which we expressed this was that, even though objectives and key concepts were common to our project, each actual piece of effective teaching must be related to four independent variables: children, teachers, schools and environments. The autonomy of the teachers is taken into account in one of these, but they also require the teacher to make a professional appraisal of the other three. All of our trials in schools have hitherto been developed in this way. The team has discussed the adaptation of objectives and key concepts within particular contexts, and an extensive range of context-specific materials, or 'units', have been built up.

When we actually come to the diffusion stage, some of these will be available as 'exemplars', to use the currently fashionable phrase. But the emphasis will be placed on teachers' own ideas and production of materials by and for them. This will in turn imply that opportunities must be afforded for them to undertake work in places such as teachers' centres or resource centres and we hope that the danger of tissue rejection may be avoided because the tissue will be not grafted, but native. All of this lies in the future and therefore a long way from the first-generation projects that we studied; but it is a direct consequence of our thinking about what we heard and observed.

This brings me to the other innovatory feature of this project about which we are still so tentative that we hardly have the audacity to mention it in public. I think it can be most readily explained in terms of our objectives. I mentioned, earlier, that we had decided only, as it were, on points, on an objectives-based approach. The cogency of the Humanities Project's arguments had left a permanent impact on our thinking, a disturbing non-objectives-based element which plagued us whenever we thought that we had devised a complete programme. It so happened that our uneasiness was exacerbated by the arrival in Liverpool last autumn of Professor A. H. (Tony) McNaughton, of Auckland University, who had not only been a key figure in the curricular developments associated with Hilda Taba in California but had actually been at Norwich with the Humanities team during the summer. In addition, he believed that effective thinking about curriculum does not depend on devising a best-fit scheme, perfecting it, and ignoring whatever does not fit in. In his view, it is essential to pay attention to just those instances that are incompatible with a tidy system, and thus to be ready to bear down intellectual edifices again and again in order to accommodate the awkward exception. The hope of establishing any complete system, even at the height of Aquinas, Spinoza, or Marx, is thus subordinated to a belief that ideas and circumstances are always changing.

It was therefore hardly surprising that Professor McNaughton urged us to dwell upon our unease about our objectives and key concepts in two ways. First, there was the danger that we might impose them on teachers. Second, even if we did not, there was the danger that any scheme of objectives on which we decided now might be obsolete in a decade. So we began to look more explicitly on our objectives and key concepts as provisional, contingent, rather than fixed or basic. But in that case it became necessary to think closely about the role of the objectives and key concepts that we had provisionally drawn up. There was in fact no difficulty about justifying their use for the duration of the schools trials: for that purpose, they had the status of a treaty between partners. But for the permanent legacy of the project, they will not do.

It is important to make quite clear why they will not do. It is not because we consider that they are themselves likely to be totally inappropriate. On the contrary, a reasoned prognosis might well be that something like our lists would be drawn up by any other professionally-qualified group within, say, the next five years. We

D

are not apologetic about our lists, even though we are not ready to nail our colours to them. The real objection is of a quite different kind, namely that the essential element is not the lists themselves but the act of thinking them out and, even more than that, the recognition that the act of thinking them out is critically important. The phrase that we like to use for this purpose is that teachers should think 'deeply, systematically, and reflectively' about what they are doing. If we have a single aim that we wish to render permanent, it is this. It will also be the major goal of our diffusion programme. And it is the contribution that we should like to think we are making to curriculum development in general.

Our diffusion programme does not begin until the autumn of 1973 and so we have still to encounter the innumerable practical problems which it is bound to generate. But we are well aware that one and a half years have elapsed since we began – nearly three years since our project was first mooted – and that curriculum development has itself moved on during that time. The establishment of a Schools Council Working Party on dissemination, for example, exemplifies a wider official recognition that projects do not perpetuate their innovations automatically. The transition from large, central, projects like ours to a more fragmented, school-based structure reflects not only (as it certainly does) the bleak financial climate of 1973 but also a healthy outcome of the first-generation projects in at least one respect, namely that local initiatives are now more feasible, and that teachers and administrators are readier to espouse them. This particular development, of course, owes a great deal to Dr Rudd's own work in the North West Project. Meanwhile, curriculum development has established itself rapidly as one of the most convincing aspects of educational studies and perhaps *the* aspect in which the necessary relation of theory to practice can be most persuasively demonstrated. The growing importance of the *Journal of Curriculum Studies* provides further evidence of this trend, which is indeed also borne out by the bringing together of the participants in this Conference. All of this reminds us that we, too, are beginning to look our age and show grey hairs.

We are therefore now led to wonder whether we, in our turn, have any specific contribution to make towards what, in these changed circumstances, could be described as third-generation developments. Summarizing what I have already said, I should certainly want to urge anyone now planning their programme to avoid over-emphasis on the production of materials and especially to avoid the appearance of laying down a complete course. Linked with this I would stress the necessity of relating any innovation to its context, and thus also of endeavouring to ensure that future developments arise – as well they may in future – from vigorous local initiatives that are nevertheless adequately grounded in strenuous and effective thinking. Finally, pursuing this last point, I would advise looking beyond methods, beyond objectives, beyond key concepts, to teachers as adequate, responsible, professionals, never complacent but never cynical, and adequately supported by the sort of ancillary help that professionals are entitled to expect. Maybe this is utopian: it may however be better than de-schooling.

To offset this venture into rhetoric, may I end with a most sober warning which I pass on from our project, the warning to which I referred earlier. It is a very mundane and prosaic one, but one that has implications for what I have said about ancillary help. It is simply that the production of any materials, however transient, involves a great deal of humdrum but concentrated effort in typing, collating, stapling and posting. We have bored to despair several teenage office girls by our demands, and owe a huge debt of gratitude to some older ladies who have been prepared to put up with our foibles. I hope that anyone else who is about to set out on a similar venture will be able to avoid this apparently trivial difficulty. Unfortunately, I have never yet met anyone who did. And it is necessary to contrive these matters before attempting immortality.

References

BLYTH, W. A. L., DERRICOTT, R., ELLIOTT, G., SUMNER, HAZEL M. and WAPLINGTON, A. (1972) *History, Geography and Social Science 8–13: An Interim Statement* Obtainable from School of Education, University of Liverpool, PO Box 147, Liverpool L69 3BX

ENNEVER, L. F. and HARLEN, WYNNE (1969) *With Objectives in Mind* Schools Council *Science 5/13* Project London: Macdonald Educational

HOYLE, E. (1969/1970) 1 How does the curriculum change? 2 Systems and strategies, *Journal of Curriculum Studies*, 1, 3, 1969 Planned Organizational change in Education *Research in Education*, 3 May 1970

LAWTON, D., CAMPBELL, J. and BURKITT, V. (1971) Social Studies 8–13 *Schools Council Working Paper No 39* London: Evans/Methuen Educational

MCNAUGHTON, A. H. (1966) Piaget's Theory and Primary School Social Studies *Educational Review*, 19 Nov pp 24–32

STENHOUSE, L. A. (1968–9) The Humanities Curriculum Project *Journal of Curriculum Studies* 1, 1

Teachers as Curriculum Developers:
A Second-generation Viewpoint

W. G. ALLAN RUDD
University of Manchester

Some lessons from the 1960s

How long is a generation in the context of curriculum development work? A great deal depends on how one defines the term curriculum development. If this is taken in its more general sense of improving existing practice in schools, then development work is continuous rather than episodic. For teachers working on their own or in groups have always been setting themselves new aims, devising new teaching schemes and revising their day-to-day work in the light of emerging experience. For various reasons, however, the pace of such activity has since 1960 quickened to such an extent that it is convenient to think of the turn of that decade as the beginning of a new generation of effort. Now, rather more than a decade later, there are abundant signs of a new orientation in systematic development work, and this may well mark the beginning of another generation of organized effort.

As Professor Blyth has already reminded us, the Schools Council started off with major initiatives in some fields requiring urgent action as well as taking over concerns originated by subject associations and later funded by the Nuffield Foundation. The Council's own first-generation work has often shown evidence of faith in that ideology which during the 1960s paraded as a 'recognizable philosophy of education'. Child-centred, following an integrated curriculum by means of self-directed activity, with the teacher functioning primarily as an arranger of the environment rather than as an instructor – these were the corner-stones of the ideology (DES 1967, Schools Council 1967). Project leaders were sought who epitomized this philosophy *in excelsis* and it was thought appropriate to devise curriculum schemes in backroom isolation from schools until the time came for field trials, when volunteer schools were called for. Since this philosophy was believed to summarize a general and quickening trend, particularly in primary education, selection of trial schools became largely a matter of identifying 'forward-looking' teachers, and evaluation was envisaged in terms of a dialogue (generally written) between like-minded developers and teachers.

Within the past decade this relationship has changed markedly; for though it is still accepted on all sides that curriculum developers need to look to the grass roots for guidance, it is now realized that grass roots need food and water if they are to flourish. Constructive criticism of the ideology laid bare the fact that many of its educational panaceas are no more than important half-truths. Consequently, the informal, open primary school, whose merits many educationists continue to acclaim, is now seen as a very subtle setting for learning, demanding a wide range of mature professional skills if teaching is to be effective in terms of pupils' progress. During this decade also, psychological studies of children's cognitive development have encouraged curriculum developers to bolster the subjective impression made by teachers with diagnostic tests designed to assess pupils' mastery of important cognitive skills.

However, this is not the whole story of interaction between development teams and trial schools during the decade. Leaders of national projects have during this time come to realize the formative experience members of their teams enjoy through sustained, sharp dialogue among themselves. This asset has dangers as well as advantages; for, in evaluating comments and other evidence provided by teachers, developers may attribute to limitations in teacher capacity those shortcomings which are due either to teachers' unfamiliarity with the scheme under trial or to deficiencies in the scheme itself in the hands of different types of teacher. And, since the first criterion of a curriculum is that it be teachable, this realization implies closer and more effective *two-way* communication between developers and teachers during field trials. Again, the importance of those schools where field trials are held during the developmental phase of a national project is now being realized. Such schools seem to promote a seeding effect, so that over a period of years they become centres from which diffusion of information and interest fans out. In summary, therefore, it seems probable that the second generation of national projects will pay much more attention than did the first to location of field trials, will make more effective use of teacher cooperation during field trials and will specify more closely the intended outcomes of curriculum schemes.

A second change of emphasis relates to the definition of curriculum. A decade ago it was common to define curriculum as 'planned learning experience'; now the question is being asked, 'Whose plan?' A concept of curriculum which limits the term to a *post hoc* account of teaching is of little value, for curriculum should surely play *some* part in guiding teaching. At the same time a useful concept of curriculum must leave room for creativity and individual style in teaching method, as well of course as for individual differences among pupils. Accordingly, there has emerged a newer definition of curriculum as a structured series of intended learning outcomes, the output of a curriculum development system and the input into a teaching system (Johnson 1967). In other words, a curriculum prescribes (or at least anticipates) the *results* of teaching; but it does not prescribe the *means*, i.e. the activities, materials or teaching content to be used in achieving these results. Where this definition is adopted it should go far towards resolving anxieties often expressed during the past decade lest national schemes of curriculum development constrain teacher freedom in the classroom.

Apart from national schemes, the past decade has seen the initiation of many local (often within-school) schemes. Such schemes were generally based on convictions that teaching needs to be individualized, that education is a continuing process and that it should aim for 'real understanding' including insights across the disciplines as fields of knowledge. Non-streaming, team teaching, flexible time-tabling, resource centres, independent study using multi-media materials, work experience and social service schemes are examples of innovations stemming from such ideas. However, particularly in larger secondary schools, progress with these innovations has often seemed disappointingly slow, in relation to the time and effort spent by developers, because problems of school organization, teaching methods, human relations, teaching skill, financial, material and staff resources are closely linked in large-scale curriculum reform.

One of the North West Regional Project's teacher panels monitored experiments in team teaching going ahead in 44 secondary schools. Its report (Schools Council 1974) included a cross-sectional study of the following major organizational issues, all needing resolution in eighteen of the schools studied in depth: responsibility for planning and direction; compatibility among team members; relationships between the team and other members of the staff; pupil attitudes and teacher-pupil relationships; opportunities for team consultation; importance of course content; need for adequate preparation of teaching and learning material; use of audio-visual etc. equipment; build up of resource centres and funds; and teaching accommodation.

Near the end of its review the authors comment:

Our experience forces us to recognize that new systems cannot be devised and introduced overnight. As a panel we met for one-half day per week throughout the 1968–9 school year to plan experiments in team teaching, and thus probably enjoyed more time for the task than would most staffs planning such an exercise. Yet we finished the year more aware than ever of the complex nature of this innovation. As a panel we believed (and continue to do so) that cooperative teaching can achieve many outcomes difficult to attain when teachers work in isolation, and that these goals are vitally important in the education of the less-able adolescents. Yet in itself team teaching is merely an aspect of school organization, which enables a particular range of teaching techniques to be used. The teaching techniques are themselves but means to an end, the latter being describable in terms of pupils' all round development. And only when the complete articulation is established and functioning efficiently will it be possible to test our belief in the possibility of achieving the outcomes we have in mind. To state that in none of the schools studied in our experiments were these conditions even remotely realized implies no criticism whatsoever of the strenuous efforts made during the experimental year. . . .

Given that the introduction of team teaching is a relatively long-term process, it follows that the most important resources for it are sustained energy, insight and commitment on the part of the innovators. And given that the teaching force is for the most part made up of ordinary, average human beings, from where are these attributes to come? Are schools to be driven to calling in the services of specially-trained and experienced 'change agents,' or to build up the needed head of steam by sending teachers off for some particularly inspiring course of instruction in the arts of innovation? Or is there a regenerative element in curriculum development, which more than offsets its laborious aspect by providing a sense of satisfaction in achievement and an incentive to press on further with the innovation? Though perhaps all three types of energizer are needed, we can testify as a panel to the efficacy of the last, which in greater or less degree we have all experienced.

One way of overcoming the labours and disappointments of do-it-yourself curriculum development in local contexts is for schools to work together in writing outline teaching schemes, which each school then adapts to its own circumstances. This was one of the ideas underlying establishment of local teachers' centres; but here again results have been generally disappointing, though during the past five years these centres have served several other useful functions. Perhaps more successful, because better-endowed, has been the North West Regional Project, a consortium of fifteen teachers' centres established and maintained jointly by thirteen LEAs. In particular, this project succeeded in supporting while in no way controlling teachers' efforts; in rooting development work in classroom experience; in producing teaching schemes which major publishing houses have accepted for publication; and in accumulating professional skill in curriculum development which its possessors have used subsequently in other teachers'-centre or school-based development schemes.

Against these achievements must be recorded certain important difficulties which emerged during the project. First, though all seven of the project's panels were concerned with the same age and ability levels of pupils, once course writing began each panel concentrated all its energies upon its own scheme, so as to achieve its goal within the time available. Thus substantial overlaps and gaps are apparent when schemes are considered in conjunction. This deficiency also reflects panels' unwillingness (and inability) to mark out beforehand the main structure of the whole curriculum the pupils concerned were to be offered. This difficulty is not confined to the North West Project; for the Schools Council has not yet produced any blueprint indicating, even in outline, relationships among its various offerings for any one stage in education.

Another difficulty lay in the method of teacher recruitment and in the pattern of release from schools for the work. Development activity extended over five school years, was based on use of volunteers released from their schools for one day each week, and offered the opportunity for withdrawal or recommitment at the end of each school year. This system had distinct advantages, notably in sustaining an appropriate balance between experience and enthusiasm within panels. But, whatever its virtues, the use of volunteers meant that panel members came as individuals from schools; and their ability to disseminate within their own schools ideas acquired from the project depended upon the quality of their personal relationships with school colleagues and on their status in the staff hierarchy.

A third important problem focuses on the fact that teacher panels made less use than might have been expected of the services which such specialists as LEA advisers, HM inspectors, Schools Council officers, university staffs and educational technologists could offer. In part this neglect was due to a natural tendency for those who are hard pressed for time to settle for inclusion in their schemes of teaching materials and techniques which from their experience they know will work. The pattern of weekly meetings also contributed to this situation by making it difficult for such specialists to attend meetings on any regular basis.

However, candour compels us to recognize another difficulty, which might be summed up in the following statement made by a panel member : 'For the first time a group of teachers has been given the opportunity and the resources needed to develop its own teaching schemes, and by God we're going to show them!' The element of defensiveness implicit in this statement was occasionally made explicit even towards project officers. Sometimes when the director visited a panel a member would ask, 'Have you come to tell us what to do?' The remark was always made half-humorously, but the tone in which the question was asked indicated either relief that in an emergency an authoritative figure was on hand to take over, or suspicion that teacher freedom would be constrained when the crunch came. It is important not to overstress the negative aspects of this anxiety, for it also had positive aspects. Indeed, the situation often seemed to the author strikingly similar to that shown by a young child when he first realizes that a new skill is *just* within his grasp. Despite his own bumbling efforts the child rejects all offers of adult help, and instead feverishly experiments until he can carry through the skill unaided. Willingness to admit weakness and to ask for guidance then become relatively mature responses, made only when the child's sense of personal achievement will not be demolished by accepting help. And in the North West Project many educationists other than teachers *did* contribute to project schemes. But almost all such contributions were made at a late stage in the project, both in response to an initiative taken by a panel member facing a specific difficulty, and informally on a basis of earlier acquaintance.

Constraint and innovation

Without doubt the major outcome of the past decade's development work has been increased recognition of the importance of the classroom as a focus for curriculum effort. In a general sense it has always been realized that all schools differ. What is new is the awareness of the complexity of the problem of organizational reform, whether that task be thought of in terms of grafting innovatory ideas and practices onto an existing organization, or as overcoming that inertia which prevents the organization from adjusting itself to changing circumstances.

Some dimensions of the problem are illustrated in Figure 1. Among the constraints listed, *teacher anxiety* refers both to the stresses experienced by individuals as new schemes are being worked out in a school, and to interpersonal tensions which may arise between the innovators and other members of the school staff. *Project material* includes both availability of the equipment and materials needed for innovation and the extent to which those who are expected to innovate understand concepts exemplified in the materials. *Planning resources* refers to provision of opportunity for planning within the school, and also to the availability of sufficient flexibility in time-tabling for the scheme which emerges to be incorporated into working practice. *Teaching skill* refers to practitioners' command of all the strategies needed for the proposed innovation to stand any chance of being successful and *accommodation* covers any constraints attributable to the physical setting into which the innovation is to be introduced.

Figure 1. Organizational Patterns and Innovation

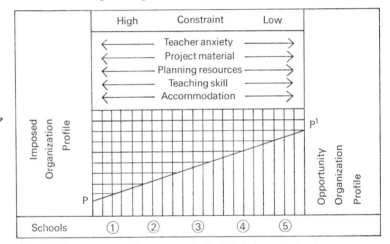

Note The figure suggests that no organization is totally constrained or entirely unconstrained.

The profile P———P[1] illustrates five different sets of circumstances. The staff of school 1, a high constraint school, are very anxious about the effects of introducing new project material chosen by an outsider (the headmaster) for their use, and which they understand only superficially. Planning time is limited by difficulty in assembling all teachers concerned (one being a married woman with young children), and because examination classes have to be kept working at full stretch while the innovation is under consideration. The department also includes a teacher who, though solid and reliable in orthodox settings, is rather set in his ways and unlikely to learn easily any needed teaching skills which he does not already possess. In this situation the departmental head will have in mind primarily the need to allay colleagues' anxieties during the early months of innovation, and so to avoid traumatic experiences in the classroom. He will therefore introduce the innovation only when a specific teaching programme has been fully worked out, which takes into account the constraints listed above. But security is achieved only at a price; and in this situation the innovation is likely to be at best only partially successful because the teachers will have only limited capacity to cope with unexpected situations as these arise during the course.

Type 3, where a medium degree of constraint operates, might represent a different institution from school 1; but let us suppose instead that it represents school 1 at the end of the first year of innovation. By this time the department staff are much more familiar than previously with the new materials, which they have discussed informally among themselves and with the departmental head at various times during the year. Though not an unqualified success, some parts of the course went well, perhaps because the staff concerned became excited by pupils' response to the materials. The examination candidates are still there, demanding attention; but the married woman has invited the other members of the department to come to her house for a few out-of-school planning sessions. The stolid conventionalist has agreed to exchange classes on occasion with the head of department, so as to be able to contribute to the scheme from his strength and to have his weakness offset. A measure of success in coping with the innovation, coupled with a feeling of shared enterprise carefully nurtured by the departmental head, has given rise to greater professional confidence in innovating. Now it becomes advantageous to relax the constraints imposed by a tight teaching programme, and to substitute instead a general agreement that by certain fixed dates in the school year particular sections of the work will be completed.

Type 5 may represent a yet more relaxed stage of school 1 than did type 3. Currently, however, institutions of type 5 are generally primary (even infant) rather than secondary schools. The most noticeable feature of this type of setting is the teachers' confidence in their own ability to respond productively to any initiative pupils may make. This confidence rests essentially on their thorough understanding of concepts and values exemplified in the materials available for study, and this mastery allows them to encourage individual pupils to select their own topics for study. Detailed teaching schemes are rarely in evidence. Instead, the teacher contrives to help each pupil at critical moments during learning activity, and at such times uses an extensive repertoire of teaching strategies to extend the pupil fully. Where accommodation problems exist the teacher does not hesitate to make use of any available corner inside or outside the classroom as a study area. Rather surprisingly, a not inconsiderable number of excellent 'opportunity-oriented' teachers show some anxiety when other adults are present in their classrooms.

While the list of variables discussed in this illustration is not exhaustive, it covers many of the schools for which innovations are currently being proposed. How, during the next few years, are curriculum developers to handle such constraints?

Needed professional skills
Without doubt the new generation of national projects will benefit from the experience of its predecessors. However, important as such benefit is, it is less critical in the current context than the need for focusing attention on the school itself as a curriculum development centre. One statistic alone is sufficient to justify this assertion. During the next twelve months the Schools Council expects to publish the products of no less than 28 of its first-generation projects; and teachers will concurrently be bombarded also with many other new and attractive materials. If the products of all these efforts are not to be lost without trace, schools must develop the professional skills needed to evaluate and adapt the materials for themselves and, particularly, to devise effective teaching schemes based on the materials they choose to adopt. Unless this happens the materials will languish on the shelves of warehouses or stock cupboards, grim reminders of unwise outlay and wasted effort.

By now it is not difficult to identify the professional skills needed for curriculum reform in schools. Essentially, there are four:

1 a substantial measure of understanding of the educational (cognitive, affective and skill) content embodied in each of the several kits competing for adoption;
2 skill in systematically planning, trying out, evaluating and improving new study sequences;
3 group functioning skill, needed wherever teachers are to cooperate in evaluating newly available materials, in planning or in teaching new courses;
4 an extended repertoire of specific teaching techniques called for by the new materials, new goals and new organizations within school.

As we shall see, these skills can probably best be developed in association. To put the same point another way, the best context for learning these professional skills is the local development project.

Activity might well begin with the local teachers' centre leader organizing a function to draw some newly-published materials to the attention of a defined group of teachers known to be interested (for one reason or another) in updating its teaching schemes. To lead this function, an educationalist should be available who is familiar with the aims and rationale of the project which produced these materials. At this point the first problem arises; for local centre leaders in all parts of the country will be seeking qualified speakers at about the same time, i.e. when teachers wish to hear about the newly-published materials. It follows that *during the pre-publication period for these materials* the Schools Council should hold orientation courses for educationalists, already well-qualified in the curriculum area concerned, who are likely to be called upon for such functions.

The well-prepared teachers' centre leader will have a few copies of key parts of the new curriculum materials available for interested volunters from the audience to take away *immediately* for trial in their schools, on condition that they will report back on the outcomes of these trials. This may serve a second purpose when, with luck, teachers report varying degrees of success with the same teaching materials. Well chaired, this meeting should lead to clarification of the project's aims and methods, and to an *ad hoc* discussion of ways of judging whether or not these are capable of being achieved.

The next stage, that of systematic local experiment, is crucial in two respects. First, motivation in the schools concerned is vital; and this is likely to be substantially higher where a school appreciates that it is experimenting on behalf of colleagues in other schools as well as for its own benefit. Second, it is essential *at this stage* to involve all educationalists whose support will eventually be needed if the experiment is to stand a chance of succeeding. Prominent among these will be the head teacher, departmental heads (where appropriate) and LEA advisers. Sometimes members of university or college of education staffs may have specific skills which the experimenters need.

Lack of space precludes a full statement of the sequence of steps involved in translating resource materials into working schemes, *carrying through an experiment and evaluating its outcomes*. For a full statement of these steps see Taba 1962. Suffice it to state that in all such work there exists a double agenda, dealing respectively with achievement of the task itself and with maintenance of morale among developers during the period of the experiment. As a general principle it is wise to divide the work from the outset into a sequence of steps, each planned for completion by a specified date; achievement of intermediate targets boosts morale and sustains commitment during an extended period of concentrated planning and experiment.

Supporting teacher initiative
Though specialist help may be needed at any stage in an experiment, it is often most needed when the range of teaching strategies has to be increased. The missing skills may be of any type, but not infrequently in secondary schools they are those related to the extension of pupils' affective powers, particularly the techniques of using class discussion to stimulate study of values. Here micro-teaching techniques might prove useful, particularly those where a teacher can analyse his own performance against some recorded model procedure.

There is one major problem of organization for innovation within schools which should not be excluded from this discussion by shortage of space. The North West Project succeeded in giving support without controlling teachers' efforts to cooperate in planning new courses; but it achieved this by locating development work on the neutral ground of a teachers' centre, and – unintentionally – at the cost of excluding much of the specialist support available in the region. It countered this defect by publishing its products in the form of highly-structured courses, which it believed would help teachers who were trying to innovate in tightly-constrained settings. However, during the next generation of local development schemes it will be important to quicken the pace of innovation by locating systematic development activity within individual schools. It will also be important to make available specialist help wherever and whenever that help is needed, *yet without seriously limiting schools' freedom and responsibility for curriculum decision.*

To achieve these goals calls for professional skill of a very high order among those invited to give specialist support, and an unusually high degree of professional confidence among those teachers playing central roles in the experiments. HM Inspectorate has a long and distinguished experience of offering suggestions and information to teachers in informal settings, and LEA advisers often use a similar style of support very effectively. However, such advice can more easily be accepted in the relaxed 'opportunity-based' school environments, which are in any case less difficult climates for innovation.

The problem thus resolves itself into one of supporting key

personnel who wish to innovate in highly or fairly highly constrained school environments, without seriously undermining their autonomy of action. Doubtless several ways of offering such support will occur to the reader, depending on the special circumstances of each setting for innovation. One general scheme which commends itself to the author is to involve a group of schools in parallel development exercises, each planning its own teaching scheme but using the same resource materials and support services as other schools in the consortium. Development work would then take place in two types of settings: within each school under leadership of the departmental head concerned; and across the district in a panel comprising only heads of the appropriate departments in each of the participating schools. New information, ideas and suggestions would generally be put forward in district meetings, thereby permitting interpretation in the light of circumstances specific to each school. Moreover, in district meetings departmental heads would have opportunities for discussing among themselves the strengths and weaknesses of each suggestion offered. Such a scheme might also appeal to the specialists concerned, for it offers an economical way of supporting the efforts of a substantial number of schools.

Head teachers and departmental heads are key members of any school's staff, and this proposal depends heavily on the likelihood of enlisting their enthusiasm and initiative for the innovation. The hard truth is that we now recognize the importance of the time dimension in innovation, and that sustained energy and commitment are needed if new schemes are to flourish. Thus, wherever departmental heads derive regeneration of enthusiasm from their district meetings this will serve as motive power for them and their colleagues to draw upon during within-school efforts.

In the author's view, therefore, the second generation of school-based curriculum development efforts should focus on consortia, each of about fifteen neighbouring schools, all working on common problems and all supported by the specialist help needed if they are to effect their innovations. Since many key educationalists in the area of each consortium will be involved in its work, each such venture will require careful planning, sound leadership and adequate secretarial, etc, resources. In most parts of the country this recommendation adds up to a call for positive discrimination in favour of innovating schools for a period of, say, three years. The author believes this to be justified; for, wherever successful, it ought to yield two important fringe benefits in addition to the innovations themselves. First, those schools which succeed in stabilizing their innovatons could serve as models for other schools to visit when planning innovation. Second, those who weather the storm of the innovation project will have at their disposal a range of professional skills which they can easily adapt to other tasks – and which they could help other colleagues to develop.

If, within the next five years, each LEA in the country could establish one primary and one secondary school consortium, and could carry through in it even *one* successful innovation, second-generation local development movement would become firmly established, and the outlook for third-generation curriculum development would be very bright indeed.

References

DES (1967) Children and Their Primary Schools *The Plowden Report* London: HMSO

JOHNSON, M. (1967) Definitions and Models in Curriculum Theory *Educational Theory* pp. 127–40

SCHOOLS COUNCIL (1967) Society and the Young School Leaver *Working Paper No 11* London: HMSO

SCHOOLS COUNCIL (in press) *Experiments in Team Teaching* London: Macmillan ch. 5

TABA, H. (1962) *Curriculum Development: Theory and Practice* New York: Harper and Row, Ch. 20

Section 2: Curriculum Courses in Colleges and Universities

Introduction

DOUGLAS BARNES
University of Leeds

Richard Pring's *Curriculum Courses: An Interdisciplinary Failure* had its context in the section of the conference that was devoted to the discussion of courses in curriculum studies at colleges and universities. In it he looks critically at some assumptions upon which existing courses are based, and suggests areas of dispute which should be central to any course, however elementary.

In a second paper David Jenkins distinguished prescriptive 'models for' curriculum from descriptive 'models of' curriculum. It became clear in discussion that courses can similarly be divided according to the view of curriculum that they present to students, in the following way:

1 Curriculum Studies as a Problem-Solving Methodology:
Students soon have to go into schools and plan lessons and join in team-teaching, so they should be provided with systematic methods for identifying their tasks and carrying them out. The methods recommended were usually those that Richard Pring calls 'the Rational Curriculum Plan' – objectives, content and learning experiences, and evaluation.

2 Curriculum Studies as a Description of Curricular Realities:
Every curriculum is context-bound: to understand a curriculum it is necessary to understand the social context in which it is enacted – the organizations and the expectations and values of the people acting in them.

Both speakers saw a danger that prescriptive models for curriculum might impose unrealistic preconceptions which were inferior to the intuitive understanding that students brought to the course. A model might 'screen out some of the messages', (as David Jenkins put it), so that the students would ignore the hidden curriculum communicated by the social norms of the school. Like Professor Hirst, Jenkins thought that parts of curriculum might never be fully open to analysis; he recommended a stance of 'not knowing quite'.

Richard Pring too questioned the emphasis placed upon 'objectives' in the Rational Curriculum Plan, because by ignoring the interpretative activity of the learner, and the changing goals of the teacher in the light of this activity, 'it provides a false and misleading model of the educational process.' Although the word 'objectives' became the focus for heated exchanges in discussion, what was in question was the nature of education, and the nature of the teacher's responsibilities. 'Under the rug of technique lies an image of man,' as Elliot Eisner once wrote.

In criticizing the Rational Curriculum Plan, David Jenkins put in a plea for 'the unstable but eclectic arts of the performer' – the intuitive knowledge and judgments necessary to a teacher – and during the discussion others suggested that there was often little relationship between teachers' stated aims and their actions. This was open, however, to the retort that curriculum studies sought to encourage an increase in rational responsibility which this showed to be necessary.

Were students in initial training capable of looking at curricula in action, and understanding the complex interaction of organizational and ideological pressures? They needed a methodology to make sense of what they saw. Yet this methodology could direct their eyes away from points of dispute. David Jenkins argued for 'high-risk courses' which would face students with controversial issues: for example, planning by means of objectives would be presented as a matter of dispute, not as part of an unquestioned methodology. He had just returned from Chicago where he had observed an 'open school', in which learning had moved out of a special institution and into the community, with the help of members of the community other than teachers. He doubted whether any existing curriculum model could do justice to what he had seen.

All students, even those in initial training, have knowledge of curriculum from being pupils themselves. What value should be placed upon this knowledge? One member put forward the case for sharpening students' 'awareness' by encouraging them to look critically at their own education so as to order and make explicit their intuitive knowledge. This contrasted sharply with the belief that students need the support of a methodology before they can be expected to make sense of a curriculum. We were revisiting the familiar debate about the relative value of the publicly ordered knowledge of a discipline in comparison with the intuitive knowledge of the learner.

But what existence has Curriculum Studies as a discipline? Richard Pring hinted that it could be described as theories expanding why other theories are bad. If it is about anything it is about educators collaborating with one another, and needing common ground on which to communicate. Most curriculum courses in colleges and universities have been marred by the 'interdisciplinary failure' of psychologists, sociologists and philosophers to find a common frame of reference. David Jenkins saw curriculum studies as political, arising from attempts by some groups to take over power from others. 'Physician, heal thyself!' seemed an appropriate injunction. Our own discussions – though they were sometimes rational – showed little similarity to Rational Curriculum Planning. Perhaps Curriculum Studies is no more than a pseudo-discipline, a whistling in the dark at a time of change and uncertainty.

Uncertainty seemed embodied in the great diversity of courses being taught. Some colleges, faced with hundreds of students, could do little more than give lectures which might help students when they went on school practice. When there were only a few students, and those experienced teachers, it was possible to carry out descriptive studies in schools or to work with development projects. One college emphasized published curriculum materials, such as *Man: a Course of Study*, and arranged for students to collaborate with teachers in exploring the uses of these materials. There was a general desire to relate theoretical discussion of curriculum with the actualities of schools but this was often frustrated by lack of access to information and to schools. A course on curriculum could not remain content with a context-free methodology, but must face substantive questions about what content should be taught to whom in what context, and must look critically at any justifications offered.

Curriculum Courses:
An Interdisciplinary Failure

RICHARD PRING
University of London Institute of Education

Curriculum: its practical and interdisciplinary nature
There are problems in calling education a discipline. Rather, it appears to embrace a loosely connected range of problems that individually call upon quite distinct disciplines such as philosophy, sociology, and psychology for their solution. The attempt in recent years, therefore, to make the study of education academically respectable has resulted in the separate study of these separate disciplines. There are courses in the philosophy of education, the psychology of education, and the sociology of education. Only the students, the recipients of the courses, are expected to draw, from these separate disciplines, interdisciplinary answers to interdisciplinary problems or questions.

Curriculum, as a subdepartment of educational theory, shares with the latter similar problems of identity. Curriculum questions come in all shapes and sizes. Most are fairly practical; for example, 'what mathematics should I teach 3b, given their previous teaching, etc?' Most, too, are context bound – that is, relevant to particular subject areas or to particular groups of children. For example, 'how much progress can be made in French without mastering the intricacies of certain irregular verbs?' One consequence of the practical and context-bound nature of so many curriculum questions is that the answers do not lie in anything remotely describable as general curriculum theory. And theoretical insight, where this is required, would appear to have its natural home in psychology, or sociology, or philosophy, or comparative studies, and would therefore seem to require an expert in the respective areas. The curriculum expert whose expertise is not rooted elsewhere therefore seems to be a bit of a myth.

If this is true, then an interesting exercise would be to explain the growth of this myth. One explanation, that might readily be acceptable to some, would doubtless be provided by our ethnomethodological comrades. Curriculum theory or curriculum expertise could be seen as a process of 'legitimating' (sic) the opinions of some people who happen to be in positions of control, so that they might secure that control more firmly. Thus, a lot of curriculum theory is bad, but further theory develops in order to show why it is bad; hence, a literature is built up, and an expert is the one who knows that literature, irrespective of its value. I have some sympathy with this view, though not with its illogical and extreme consequences as argued by some exponents.

Where perhaps curriculum theory differs from general educational theory is that it is concerned with a narrower range of educational problems, in which there is a genuine opportunity for the development of practical expertise and the skills or arts of linking different sorts of disciplinary contributions. For curriculum questions are in the main practical, and the practical is always an interdisciplinary undertaking, linking precepts and values with hard facts about, and (in some cases) a theoretical grasp of, a particular situation.

I make these preliminary points for the following reasons. There is a temptation (for reasons perhaps already hinted at, namely, of creating a niche in the academic world) to create a single discipline for what should essentially be an interdisciplinary approach to a loosely connected range of practical problems. This results in the following mistakes: (a) the adoption of particular models with spurious claims to relevance and intellectual respectability (as, for example, in the systemic analysis of curriculum design, illustrated in one unit of the Open University Curriculum Course, E283); (b) the failure to see the relevance of critical questions rooted in the theory of particular disciplines (as, for example, in the wholesale adoption of Bloom's taxonomy by those unaware of fairly fundamental epistemological objections); (c) the takeover bid by one discipline of essentially interdisciplinary tasks (as, for example, when philosophers appropriate the right to sort out concepts such as 'planning', 'morality', 'curriculum', 'disciplines', independently of, and indeed prior to, the field work and experience of psychologists, sociologists, teachers, etc.); and (d) the failure to temper theoretical considerations with practical insight or practical consequences (as, for example, in so much fruitless presentation of general and specific objectives as a result of purely *a priori* theorizing). I could go on. My main points, however, are: that curriculum questions are by and large practical, and are thereby interdisciplinary. They thus require for their solution the cooperation of an interdisciplinary team; and in failing to recognize this, one is in danger of creating a spurious discipline or at least of failing to give a balanced account.

What follows will simply illustrate these points in some detail and tentatively suggest a few areas in which general curriculum questions can be useful focal points for interdisciplinary cooperation.

A curriculum model

Any course in curriculum theory would at some stage expound, illustrate, and examine what has come to be known as the Rational Curriculum Plan, viz. the fourfold division of the planning process into objectives, content, method, and evaluation. Not only might this be seen as a sensible breakdown of any planning process, but it might provide a useful way of dividing up a course (or indeed a textbook) concerned with general curriculum theory (look, for example, at Wheeler's *The Curriculum Process*, 1967). Thus, assuming that any rational activity must be clear about the end of the activity, curriculum planners will assume as self-evident the need for objectives; and recognition of this need concentrates the mind on preliminary questions about the sources of objective. (It is at this stage that the philosopher, as an expert in value judgments, will be introduced!). Both content and method will largely be the concern of psychologists for, after objectives have been decided upon, is not the choice of means (viz. content and method) by which these objectives are reached a purely contingent matter, that is, something open to empirical enquiry? Clarity in the original statement of objectives will render evaluation comparatively straightforward. The objectives either have or have not been reached. If they have, all well and good; if they have not, then either the means are inefficient or the objectives are inappropriate.

This model of curriculum design and planning is seductive in its simplicity. As I said, not only does it constitute the subject matter of some courses (something to be shown and taught), but it also provides a convenient framework for organizing courses and for raising more detailed questions within. Thus, it is asked, how precisely do objectives need to be specified? Well, the answer goes, sufficiently precisely to allow clarity of aim, choice of means and unambiguous evaluation. Moreover, it is further assumed that such clarity and precision will be achieved when objectives are finally analysed into intended student behaviours – hence the growth of literature in that direction. And of course this answer itself generates a range of questions about the classification of such objectives. The fact that Bloom, Krathwohl and others have taken the trouble to produce such a classification has been treated by many as a godsend. Not only does acquaintance with Bloom become a sizable component of a course, but it also becomes a ready-made tool for those about to engage in some form of curriculum development. In this connection it is worth examining the planning of the following Schools Council projects: History, Geography and Social Science 8–13 and the North West Regional Curriculum Development Project. There are, of course, many publications about objectives in subject areas which look upon the taxonomy as holy writ.

What I have sketched in a very broad outline is the general shape of a curriculum course as many conceive it. It is too broad and too familiar to make my account of any interest in itself. What is of interest is the way in which its adoption, in different guises and with different modifications, reflects a failure to recognize the practical and inter-disciplinary nature of curriculum questions. To illustrate this, I suggest the following ways in which this course has failed:

1 by ignoring certain philosophical questions, it is theoretically mistaken;
2 by arguing from theory to practice, (e.g. in being too theoretical in some cases), it is practically useless.

These basic inter-disciplinary failures can of course be subdivided and added to. I shall do this to some extent. But my main task is to illustrate a point.

Interdisciplinary failure illustrated

Failure to see philosophical questions
Relevant philosophical questions might be posed (but frequently are not) at three different points in a curriculum plan: (a) the specification of objectives, (b) their classification, and (c) the relationship of content and method to these objectives. I shall discuss each of these in turn.

(a) It is assumed as self-evident, and rarely argued, that to act intentionally, let alone rationally, one must have objectives. Moreover, greater efficiency and clarity are possible if, beforehand, these objectives are made explicit. First decide where you are going, and then, in the light of existing evidence and experience, decide how you are going to get there.

Now this rather simple model of intentional activity does not stand up to too close a philosophical scrutiny. In brief, it ignores the interpretative activity of the learner (or the interpretative activity of the teacher who is the recipient of the curriculum plan) and it ignores the changing definition of goals in so far as either the teacher or the pupil is engaged in an intellectual pursuit. In other words, because it ignores the fact that teachers or children are autonomous, thinking persons, it provides a false and misleading model of the educational process.

Much more could be said about this and needs to be said if it is to become a convincing argument. But I raise the point by way of illustration, and by way of pointing out characteristic failures of some curriculum courses. The failure lies, firstly, in not presenting

71

the alternative view in an area that is essentially controversial. I believe the only honest way to deal with issues in a controversial area is to show both sides of the argument. Secondly, it lies in not providing the framework within which much valuable curriculum development and design becomes intelligible (for example, the Keele Integrated Studies Project, the Humanities Curriculum Project, and the Nuffield Junior Science Project – all of which I shall examine in greater detail later).

These observations for curriculum courses point up the need not only to represent different points of view but also to be sensitive to critical questions rooted in different theoretical approaches. These can be achieved only within an interdisciplinary framework and by the awareness of problems as they confront the curriculum practitioner. Of course it helps, too, to have some acquaintance with decent educational literature. Beauchamp, Mager, and Popham could be profitably juxtaposed with certain choice extracts from Dewey, who had some interesting things to say about objectives.

(b) It is, of course, a small step from arguing the need for specific objectives to attempting to clarify them. Clearly, the more specific one is in setting out objectives, the more objectives one finds which require classification. There are, however, important philosophical questions to be raised about logical divisions of objects, events, or achievements. This is especially the case where achievements are mental. Quite a lot of people since Plato have spent time discussing such questions.

One worrying feature of curriculum courses, and of curriculum planning and design, has been the uncritical, and therefore in my view, mistaken application of a taxonomy of objectives. Again, it is not my job to say here in detail why it is mistaken. Roughly my reasons would centre round the artificial distinctions between cognitive and affective domains, and secondly the quite erroneous distinctions between knowledge, comprehension, application, etc., within the cognitive domain. But the point of my illustration does not depend upon the strength of my argument, but upon the recognition of an important area of controversy. And so long as there remain these critical questions, the taxonomy cannot be regarded as a sort of blueprint to be universally and uncritically applied across the curriculum board. It removes flexibility in approach (the cognitive/affective distinctions determine how one is to conceive things, rather than providing a tool for analysis) and it precludes the raising of critical questions within an ongoing situation.

(c) It is common, in theoretical talk about planning, first to determine the goals, and then to decide upon the means by which

72

these goals might be achieved. How to get there is decided, in the light of experience, by the content to be chosen, the methods to be adopted, the organization to be arranged, the resources to be collected.

Upon examination, however, the relationship of means to end is much more complicated than that. The end logically limits what is to constitute appropriate means, and indeed, where the end is seen (as it frequently is in education) as an ongoing activity rather than a particular product, the distinction between means and end becomes very fuzzy indeed.

If this is correct, then much of the work concerning the adoption of appropriate means is logical rather than empirical. It requires as much conceptual analysis as it requires empirical investigation, and it requires as much expertise within the specific activity as it requires the expertise of general curriculum theory. The adoption of means is very much an interdisciplinary task, requiring the continual posing of critical questions. The actual stage at which particular questions need to be asked cannot be anticipated. The whole thing must be an integrated enterprise.

The practical experience of curriculum design and development gives the lie to the stage by stage division of the curriculum process. Let us take just one example. A naive interpretation of the Humanities Curriculum Project would see certain questions about teaching strategies (for example, the teaching role of procedural neutrality) to be about the empirical relationship of means to the attainment of certain ends. But the reality is interestingly different from that. Firstly, the attempt to define this role has proved not only difficult but also illuminating. It has raised important philosophical and ethical questions about teaching, indoctrination, knowledge, responsibility, etc., which have affected the very conception of the project as a whole. Secondly, this critical examination of the teaching role was not something that could be located in some one stage of the project; it was co-terminous with this development. Thirdly, this critical examination, although in one sense philosophical, could not be isolated from empirical work within classrooms – how teachers work, what conditions they work in, how teachers conceive their role in different wide social frameworks, etc. Such non-philosophical background not only provides criteria of relevance for philosophical examination; it becomes the very stuff which enters into philosophical reflection. Of course, this has interesting consequences for philosophy of education courses: analyses of the teaching concept seem like so many interesting games when played in isolation from actual issues posed in a non-philosophical way. But my major point here is that the complex interrelationship between means and end cannot be anticipated at the onset of the particular curriculum development, but must itself be a critical part of that development, requiring, therefore, continual interdisciplinary cooperation.

Take-over bid by one discipline (e.g. philosophy)
An alternative to ignoring philosophy is to require too much from it. Thus it is interesting to see how, in some courses and in some examinations, the philosophical dissection of disciplines, 'forms of knowledge', concepts of teaching or 'morality', etc., opens the field to the psychologist or the sociologist. Thus, in general educational theory (especially at B.Ed. level), disciplinary isolation is supposedly overcome by set pieces from a triumvirate consisting of philosopher, psychologist, sociologist. The philosopher sets the pace because it is his job to dissect the concept or topic, and to ask the psychologist and the sociologist for the relevant empirical evidence. The failure of this interdisciplinary attempt is due to the perversity of the social scientists, who may not like the questions the philosopher has asked, and prefer to pose their own. In addition, the very nature of many education courses prevents even this level of cooperation. Thus, in the philosophy of education course, questions about curriculum content will be posed in purely philosophical terms, thereby giving the impression that purely philosophical answers will suffice. Forms of knowledge then become the same as curriculum subjects, which I do not think they were ever intended to be. (An afterthought: to what extent has the extinction of Farmington man been due to philosophical imperialism?).

The main difficulty here is the false view that philosophy can go it alone – that in isolation from non-philosophical pursuits it can provide some sort of blue print – idealized perhaps; in need of modification to meet particular circumstances, perhaps; but relevant and practical for all that. For example, it might, by some, be argued stage by stage as follows: the very concept of rational action requires a clear conception of the end of action (what is intended); these ends should be spelt out in terms of desirable states of mind; possible desirable states of mind will be derivable from epistemological analysis of knowledge and its differentiation; actual desirable states of mind will depend on essentially ethical analysis of what is of most worth, the whole thing constitutes a logic of curriculum. (Of course in practice the desirable will be restricted by the possible, and that will in part be an empirical matter.)

There are many ways in which one might seek to expose this *a priori* approach to curriculum questions. I am beginning to prefer the full frontal exposé – namely the argument, not simply that this is bad philosophy, but that it is not doing the sort of job philosophy

74

ought to be doing. That it is bad philosophy arises from the inadequate analysis of 'rational action', and from the way in which it dominates the conception one has of a discipline (think of the contortions undergone by those students who try to fit English into a form of knowledge or who seek the distinctive concepts of music or the verification procedures in works of art). But more fundamental is the criticism that this is not the job philosophy should be doing. Good philosophy has never isolated itself from the empirical workers in the field, and philosophy of education will be impoverished if it does not arise out of the problems posed by non-philosophical field workers.

Let us take one example, that of the concept of a discipline. Entering into this analysis must be the socio-historical perspective that has helped to demarcate certain territories – it is not just a logical or epistemological analysis that is required. And the maintenance of distinctions might receive some insight from a more general analysis of the social and institutional structure of academic life. Yet it has frequently been the unquestioned assumption of education and curriculum courses that this aspect of the content of curriculum is the peculiar province of philosophy.

I have made two very general points to illustrate my theme of interdisciplinary failure in curriculum course: on the one hand, the uncritical adoption of too simple a model (which makes it philosophically inadequate); and on the other, the domination of curriculum question by one discipline, (which overweights it philosophically). In making these points, I have constantly referred to the practice of curriculum design and development. It would be useful to put these references into some sort of order. Thus we may ask ourselves what sort of validity a course in curriculum can have unless it is continually brought up against the exigencies of curriculum practice.

Need for examination of curriculum practice
I wish briefly to refer to three curriculum projects. Two questions need to be borne in mind. Am I right in what I say about them? Does what I say have the consequences I outline – in particular, consequences for curriculum courses?

Nuffield Junior Science Project
This project, carried out in consultation with teachers, produced materials that would help them (the teachers) to exploit everyday situations about which the children raised questions. It was an attempt to prepare materials for unpredictable situations, to define general principles for handling these situations, to come to some

practical understanding of these principles within the given group of schools, and to devise ways of communicating what happened. Note, in particular, that in no way did either the project directors or indeed the participants attempt to define precise objectives. The concept of science was loosely defined as a way of proceeding rather than in terms of particular ends to be achieved. Practical problems encountered lay in the communication of general principles and in the continuation of what had been achieved after the dispersal of the project.

Integrated Studies Project
This project also produced materials that would help teachers explore certain general themes (e.g. man the explorer) in order to show, among other things, how the disciplines are integrated. It was initially worked out in conjunction with participating teachers and there was a gradual development of principles by which materials should be handled. Note, once again, that there was no definition of precise objectives to be obtained or even what precisely were the logical relations to be perceived when disciplines were integrated. Indeed, there was no clear definition of principles either. But there were considerable practical difficulties encountered. Initial failure to clarify principles led to a changing definition of key concepts (e.g. integration) and of the underlying principles. There was apparently a breakdown of communication, and a consequent failure of genuine innovation. A study in depth of these developments and those shortcomings would illuminate many central curriculum questions – as I hope briefly to indicate in my final section.

Humanities Curriculum Project
Everyone is doubtless familiar with the work of Stenhouse and his team. The aim of the project was to offer to schools and to teachers stimulus, support and materials appropriate to enquiry-based courses which cross the traditional boundaries between English, history, geography, religious studies, and social studies. The problem initially faced by this particular curriculum development were, in the words of the Schools Council's *Raising the School Leaving Age Working Paper No. 2* 'to give every man access to a complex cultural heritage, some hold on his personal life and on his relations with the various communities to which he belongs, some extension of his understanding of, and sensitivity towards other human beings. The aim is to forward understanding, discrimination, and judgment in the human field.' At least this was the view from which the Project's initial thinking started. But the Project consisted of a central team and participating teachers, each person independently

bringing views and perspectives to bear upon the development and the more detailed articulation of this brief. There was only a gradual definition of principles – principles concerning the rational development of enquiry based discussion, the provision and handling of evidence, the manner of coping with sensitive and controversial issues and the adoption of a procedurally neutral role.

Note again not only the absence but also the impossibility of any prespecified objectives; and note, too, that the definition of working principles was gradual, resulting from constant consultation and from constant reflection upon their brief by a group of people representing different traditions of thought. But again there were problems. Change in curriculum requires the definition of a new situation – the articulation of principles, if you like, in a way that is not necessary if one is following a tradition. But innovation, and the definition of principles, open up possibilities of misinterpretation that do not previously exist. Compounded with this source of misinterpretation was a clash between the values incorporated in the practice of the project and those embodied in much traditional practice. Hence, what this project illustrates for my purposes is: that articulation of principles rather than specification of objectives is what is often sought and that this articulation is a gradual and concurrent process rather than the initial stage of the development; that the principles evolve through consultation with participants and different specialisms rather than from a central team; and finally that there will arise separate problems of evaluation and diffusion, since, with the absence of clear objectives, what is to count as success or failure is initially rather unclear, and since, with clash of value and with constant misinterpretation, there will be many barriers to success.

I have chosen these three examples to illustrate a general point. Firstly, the experience of practitioners is quite different from what much theory would suggest. Secondly, it would seem to be necessary, in order to grasp the theoretically significant points, to have contact with the practice of curriculum. Thirdly, both the practical and the theoretical involvement in curriculum requires a constant interaction between different disciplines of thinking – the process is not divisible into stages which are the province of particular disciplines. The problems posed for curriculum courses are therefore twofold: how they can be organized so that students will get insight into practice, and how they can be organized so that representatives of different disciplines will submerge their philosophical or sociological or psychological identities in the pursuit of some common practical enterprise.

The answer to the second problem is partly institutional, and it would be useful (both as part of a course and in preparing a course) to develop detailed case studies of the breakdown of departmental distinctions (how it can be done and what happens as a result) in schools, colleges, universities and, of course, at institutes of education. The answer to the first problem of how students can be given insight into practice is not primarily institutional, although clearly it raises difficult organizational problems; it requires either the participation by the students in some group work or the detailed tutoring of individual assignments or the examination in depth of properly documented and evaluated curriculum designs, plans, or projects. Very little of the latter is in fact available. Possibly, following the evaluation study, the Humanities Curriculum Project would provide a well documented account of curriculum innovation. The development, diffusion, and evaluation of MACOS might be another example if money were made available for this purpose.

Focal areas for interdisciplinary enquiry
Finally, I wish to suggest broad areas in which not only would interdisciplinary cooperation be possible and desirable but in which there could also be constant reference to the current stock of practical experience.

The function of curriculum objectives
As I have indicated above, much of the demand for objectives seems to be misplaced. But even at the purely theoretical level much more needs to be said about aiming at objectives, about the distinction between this and acting according to principles, and about the underlying concepts of mind and of education that distinguish different kinds of appeal to objectives. (It is so easy to blur important educational differences by simply pointing to a few highly general features of intentional activity.) At the practical level some examination would be useful about the function of objectives in planning, designing, implementing curricula, or about the gradual articulation of principles through cooperative and interdisciplinary work.

The nature of curriculum activities
We customarily think of a curriculum as the sum of several subjects, but 'subject' is too diffuse a notion to be very helpful. Nonetheless some characterization is required of the diverse range of activities with which different curricula are concerned. There is a need for an interdisciplinary examination of subjects, disciplines, integration, the characteristic features of different traditions of thinking, departmental organization of educational activities, the criteria by which

different achievements are judged. But although certain general things can be said in this direction, it would be difficult to say much that is useful in curriculum terms without the experience and participation of those who practise the particular curriculum activities. Theoretical questions about integration have to do more than make a gesture (rude or otherwise) towards the practice of integration. They need to probe them – the underlying aims, concepts, and indeed motives. (For example, is the open plan system simply an administrator's ruse to get more space for the same money?)

Innovation
At every level, and from the very inception of their career, teachers are likely to be engaged in curriculum change. Can anything in general be said about problems connected with this – about breaking away from 'traditional' ways of performing and conceiving activities and 'creating new traditions' (Stenhouse)? Some curriculum development has documented its practical experience, and it would seem possible, through case studies, to formulate some hypothetical picture of what 'would happen if ... ?' However, barriers to success exist at many levels.

Diffusion
It is one thing to write the gospel, quite another to spread it. Successful curriculum design, and even implementation, frequently dies quickly or does not survive the short life of its author. There is a general problem of communication, of disseminating ideas, principles, innovation – call it what you will. An examination of this problem would of course raise questions about political and institutional control, about communication (and its breakdown) between developers and practitioners, and about the relation of practice to the language of practice.

Evaluation
There are problems of a peculiar kind in the evaluation of curriculum, in that there is need to assess or evaluate what is essentially innovatory and therefore lies outside the bounds of prevailing criteria. These are clearly not simply theoretical questions, but highly practical ones or ones that can be confronted on a course in a highly practical way – using various techniques for achieving some sort of self or group analysis of performance.

There are, of course, other areas for interdisciplinary and practical cooperation, and it would be useful at a conference such as this to suggest, list, and develop such areas. But these, I think, are crucial ones in the experience of those involved in the practice of curriculum design and development, and serve to illustrate my general point. Yet they are the very ones which get omitted from a purely theoretical approach. Or, if they are not omitted, they are approached in a manner which distorts the essentially interdisciplinary nature of the practical requirement.

Addendum

Several points arose in the discussion following my presentation of this paper which ought to be commented on. Firstly, it was argued that I did not distinguish sufficiently between curriculum analysis and curriculum planning or design. This is true, and I think this failure on my part affects some of the things I say. Furthermore, it is all too easy to talk about curriculum design, planning, analysis, and even inplementation together, as though there were not important differences in meaning between these, each raising different theoretical and practical questions.

What was generally omitted from the discussion, although it arose obliquely, was consideration of the institutional framework in which courses might develop. This point however is crucial if I am correct in insisting upon the interdisciplinary nature of these courses. Thus the difficulties in dealing with large numbers in initial training may be largely institutional – that is, (in this particular case) connected with the departmental division of even the education departments and the reluctance of individual members to risk themselves in less familiar and less certain territory. A solution to these problems therefore may lie less in personal conversion than in institutional change. And case studies of resistance to curriculum courses in particular institutions might be a useful part of the course.

Finally, the group tended to get very excited at the mention of objectives. This supports my view that there is much more to the 'objectives debate' than a verbal quarrel about the proper use of words. If this is the case, then it needs to be analysed in a course. And if the analysis does reveal educational differences, these should be shown.

References

SCHOOLS COUNCIL (1965) *Raising the School Leaving Age*, Working Paper No 2: London: HMSO

WHEELER, D. K. (1967) *The Curriculum Process* London: University of London Press

The Moving Plates of Curriculum Theory: A Speculator's Guide to Future Eruptions

DAVID JENKINS
Open University

How refreshing to write a paper for which to be ill-informed is a positive advantage. Chance your arm, said Douglas, betraying his growing interest in the psychomotor domain. Even the title of the paper occasioned disappointment. Some expected a demonstration of rotating plates balanced on vertical poles, followed by routine moralizing about the plight of the specialist in an eclectic field. Others guessed that the plates indicated a view that curriculum theorists would eventually be crushed during a narcissistic photographic session, victims of the psychometric consequences of excessive self regard – a kind of measurement self-interference. Alas my metaphor is a prosaic geophysical one: that curriculum theory stands astride huge rifts; that the smooth contours of the curriculum landscape belie giant movements beneath our feet. Future eruptions can be predicted along the margins of contiguous, but differently articulated traditions.

Although this paper is by definition ill-informed, it takes selective account of current thinking. All speculations about the future are provisional, in one sense taking an equal risk of being wrong. Since some of the predictions made here have the charm of being explicit, and are thus open to subsequent disproof, I must record my belief that being consistently wrong is a paradoxical virtue: extra-sensory imperception, no less. In one detail the tone of the future is easy to adopt: I repudiate a spurious gloss of academic footnotes. The paper of the future will surely abandon this nervous denial of a self-explaining culture. Civilized discourse is always allusive. No self-respecting coterie since Plato's *Republic* has descended to sir-name dropping. The future paper is likely to be characterized by a tone of cosy intimacy, just like Jack forgot to tell us. Let the miserable reader who so desires write his own footnotes, or hire one of the growing sprawl of footnote-compiling agencies. Those wishing to identify sources, or place references to their own work, should contact Hugh at *Cambridge Footnotes*, or David at *Hamilton Academicals*. Not now, but certainly in five years' time.

I have but four points to make: Attention all shipping in sea areas

F

Model Building, Knowledge Claims, Learning Milieux and Curriculum Evaluation. This is a gale warning.

Model building

Curriculum theorists are being urged to build bigger and better models, in spite of the view firmly held by teachers that models have something to do with cardboard lighthouses. But no; the models that the theorists have in mind are simplified versions of complex realities. Models organize experience. They help us to predict and explain.

Faced with such a harmless activity I risk appearing churlish in predicting that model building will soon be so totally discredited that it will be regarded as an illicit activity. What grounds are there for holding this assertion?

In the first place the activity of model building bestrides our fault. Already *models of* are drifting in one direction, *models for* in another. This leaves Janus-like constructs like John's 'model for curriculum theory' about to do the splits. But the problems won't be solved simply by introducing a more rigorous distinction between *models of* and *models for*. Both will be discredited, but for different reasons.

Models of will be repudiated less on the grounds of their guile than on the grounds of their impertinence. Few curriculum models can seriously offer in justification the claim that they reflect a natural order in the data under discussion. They are simplifying devices to aid interpretation. At worst they fail even to organize efficiently the data they purport to structure. Ernie, Tom and Joe recently subjected one of the conventional models, the research and development (popularly R & D) 'model of change' to empirical verification. This was an indirect result of their examining the effectiveness of demonstration centres; in doing so they tested one link in the R and D model in an operational setting. Predictably the 'model' was found wanting. 'Like any model,' they write, 'the R and D model is not entirely wrong: it simply attracts attention to the wrong variables.' Such a shame.

Other *models of* are self-consciously ideal types ('maxims') and consequently have unclear implication for what 'Triple-strike' Joe called the 'unstable but useable arts of the practitioner' in an eclectic field. An instructive example is provided by attempts to arrive at a formal statement of what is logically involved in a 'discipline of knowledge'. Such models take us away from interpretive accounts of what is crucial to any activity, and seek a spurious generality. What is at stake in asserting (or indeed denying) that literary criticism has 'no characteristic way of moving from raw data to conclusion'?

Models for will become discredited for other reasons. They will be judged increasingly to be crudely prescriptive, having a recommending rather than an explaining function. Interest will shift to examining their underlying assumptions. Ralph's *rational curriculum planning* will be seen as a theory about rationality and a theory about planning, but not as a theory about curriculum. Its assumptions will increasingly be regarded as untenable. Sorry, Ralph.

Soon as the worst offenders, and soonest to be cast into outer darkness, will be those sheep in wolves' clothing, *models of* purporting to be (or necessarily to infer) *models for*. Arthur and John explicitly turn a model of a discipline of knowledge into a model for a disciplined curriculum. Open University students entering the hall of mirrors of GPID will recall that John's goals/plans/implementation/development model begins as a description of the epistemic function and ends up as a prescription for curriculum planning. Sorry, John.

But be warned. Models can be expected to put up a good fight, unused as they are to being kicked out of bed. They will plead for mercy on the grounds that our intellectual life is organized around them. They will insinuate that we are incapable of generating ideas unless they supply little boxes for us to put them into. They will argue that their apparent rigidity is itself purposeful; that no *rigor* is possible without *mortis*. This is not to say that the rhetoric of model building will not remain as a literary device in *participant observation reports* and the other open-ended intellectual exercises (all written from a state of innocence) that will replace a formal curriculum theory. There are still householders in rural Shropshire who daub cottages with black tar in order to simulate the superficial appearance of the genuine half-timbered clobber. But the exercise will be self-consciously nostalgic, an appeal to one's sense of history. To this extent I anticipate an amnesty for models. But if the paint erodes, the house doesn't fall down.

Knowledge claims
Here the moving plates are clearly visible. On the one hand, and moving north, we have a classic tradition seduced by the notion of reliable knowledge. Reliable knowledge is represented as yielded through systems, and much intellectual effort has gone into exploring these systems. Individual disciplines are said to aspire to a structure, a syntax and a methodology (i.e. characteristic ways of moving from raw data to conclusion). Reliable knowledge is reliable because it is hooked into public *forms of knowledge* that 'by virtue of their peculiar terms and logic have expressions or statements that are testable against experience.' The testing criteria establish the

truth conditions of the propositions encountered. Thus knowledge is both public and structured by previous enquiries, although it is still possible to take Jerry's point about teaching to participants rather than spectators. This would involve inducting pupils into the methods of enquiry that produced the knowledge in the first place.

On the other hand, and moving south, we have a rather self-conscious challenge from the social phenomenologists, who elevate Alfred as their leading guru. George first taught us to see the world of objects (i.e. anything that can be named, whether concrete or abstract) as human constructs rather than self-existing identities with intrinsic natures. Also, to understand the human actor as meeting the world through an on-going process of definition. Human society appears not as an established structure but as people meeting their conditions of life. Phenomenology, as a branch of the sociology of knowledge, grew up within this perspective as a sociological critique of consciousness, concerned with the social construction of reality in general. Society, as Peter says, is a world-building enterprise. Human beings establish their identities through a series of 'conversations' in which language focalises, patterns and objectivates individual experience. This process is socially determined to the extent that the linguistic base of any society – its developed and preferred language patterns – offers to its members interpretive schemes, cognitive and moral norms, value systems and theoretically articulated world views. Knowledge is controlled or out of control, depending on one's point of view.

At first sight this process may appear to be best described in terms of the individual requiring on-going validation that the out-there world can be appropriated to himself and become, subjectively, his world. This, as Alfred asserts, is further complicated by the fact that people hold knowledge only *sufficiently*, and in a way correlating with the cultural pattern. It includes 'recipe' knowledge, a trusted hand-me-down formula for interpreting the social world. Most people see society as a field for actual or possible acts, and only secondarily as an object of thinking.

Press the issues a little further and we are faced with a dilemma based on the tension between objective and subjective reality, objective and subjective identity, structure and interpretation. Plausibility structures, in appropriate cultural circumstances, have little to do with truth tests. A system of astrology is not necessarily less plausible than a system of astronomy. Malcolm's *Study of Two Experimental Programmes at MIT* describes an experimental course that was quickly faced with questions about the borderline between academic and non-academic activity. Some staff members refused to accept that students were 'doing anything' when in fact they were 'practising yoga, reading contemporary American poetry aloud, learning to use pay telephones without paying, or talking about interpersonal relationships and themselves.'

I go along with Frank, if I understand him aright, in saying that the curriculum of the alternative society (or the alternative curricula of society) will pay little regard either to middle class definitions of 'worthwhile activities' or the logical structures of the 'forms of knowledge' argument. Fly away Peters, fly away Paul. Already we have intellectual wife-swapping, as anybody can attest who has attended those dreadful interdisciplinary conferences at which priests insist on talking about deviance and psychiatrists about sin. The science student of the future will be allowed, as a right, to make qualitative assertions about vibes. Physicist, heal thyself. We face a retreat from certainty in every conceivable field and a resuscitated belief in the possibility of purely personal knowledge – ragged, partial and incomplete.

The term 'core curriculum' will drop out of the literature. I guess this will coincide with Lawrie realizing that successive cultural analyses fail to replicate the approved menu of *core* uncertainties. By then the appeal of the subject curriculum will be purely apostolic, although still attracting the zeal of a straight-laced and high collared minority. As I see it, that leaves the activity curriculum as the sole survivor of the three alleged pure types. Back to the drawing board, Othanel, William and Harlan. We need more than one basic type.

Learning milieux

I think we must take Jim's point that schools are second hand and shoddy environments. Living in schools is essentially an inferior, vulgar, imitative, second-hand experience. Urban schools exacerbate these problems. The problem with such schools is not that they are irrelevant, but that they are not different (or irrelevant) enough. The implications have been spelled out elsewhere of schools allowing themselves to become 'information poor' in a culture that is increasingly 'information rich'. One solution is to encourage schools to enter a community role and become 'action rich'. Both the problem and the solution suggest the likelihood of a curriculum theory increasingly concerned with examining *learning in context*. The straws are already in the wind. Malcolm is arguing for 'situational analysis' as the initial stage in curriculum design. His namesake is arguing for 'learning milieu theory' as the missing link between studies of urbanism and theories about the curriculum of urban schools.

So what is the problem? Simply whether any theory of the

curriculum will be viable that does not stress the situational and institutional context in which the learning is taking place. This will be increasingly important as the conventional boundaries between school and community are re-drawn. I think the blue print for the future is contained in Fred and Donald's hypothetical community described in *A Proposal for Education in Community*. Learning will be pursued in three quite distinct contexts, the 'school' context, the 'laboratory studies' context and the 'community seminar' context.

The school context will concentrate on instrumental skills, with an equal emphasis on problem-centred learning. Laboratory studio work will involve learning through action in physical locations such as hospitals and factories. The community seminar will be a forum for discussing problems and issues of social significance and mutual concern.

A period of volatile change, particularly within unstable institutional frameworks, does not need the settled conceptual apparatus of particular theoretical formulations, whether the task is that of description or justification. I anticipate a greater flexibility, a willingness to back hunches, to experiment, to justify aspirations and programmes by reference to particular circumstances rather than universal truths. This situational morality of curriculum development will be most sharply seen in relation to curriculum evaluation. We are about to enter a new golden age for the holistic interpretive account. At the centre of this quasi-theory will be the decision makers. Their key question will be: what counts as responsible choice?

But this optimistic picture discounts a landmass moving in the opposite direction towards colder political climates; a new doctrine of accountability, and greater standardization. The word 'standardization' occurred in the account of everybody whom I asked before the conference. The premises are there: the curriculum is being viewed increasingly as a legitimate object of social policy: it is a small step from institutionalizing the process of curriculum change to holding a clear preference concerning its direction and building this into a national policy. But my guess is otherwise: that we are going to see spectacular local initiatives and that theory will increasingly become context-bound.

Curriculum evaluation

We are about to witness a paradigm shift in the field of educational evaluation in favour of a 'social anthropology' model, using the methodology of participant observation. I go along with Ernie that such evaluation will be political, used to allocate resources, cover up mistakes, build reputations and make money. It will be organized around crucial decisions and will adopt decision-makers as its principal target audience.

The new-style evaluation will in Malcolm's terminology be 'illuminative'. In the account he and David offer in their paper on *Evaluation as Illumination*, the paradigm shift involves a shift in related assumptions. Central to the understanding of illuminative evaluation are two other concepts, the *instructional system* and the *learning milieu*. The latter is the socio-psychological and material environment in which students and teachers work together. It is a network of cultural social psychological and institutional variables. Each set of circumstances is unique.

The choice facing us can again be seen fancifully as the product of pressures generated by our moving plates. I take it that the psychometric paradigm and the 'behavioral objectives' approach will survive by making more modest claims than currently espoused, although it could become, like Isambard's pneumatic railway, a neat idea that never became fully operational because of a tragic flaw in the internal logic. Elliott is an enigmatic figure in the debate. Many see him as occupying the lunatic fringe on this issue, but I am prepared to back both his 'expressive objectives' and his advocacy of the 'procedures and techniques of art criticism'. These will prove to have considerable mileage in curriculum evaluation. This new taste for criticism, for irony and metaphor; this new relishing of the absurd, will fit in easily with what participant observers will be doing when they rid themselves of the notion that social science is a science. These alternative evaluations will make entertaining reading. They will claim to be recognizable rather than true. They will be cryptic, backing Bob's notion of 'display'. Barry supposes wall charts, but they may be communicated in other ways, printed along school chalk or even as edible messages in Schools Council rock. Whatever happens, and in the best sense of the term, evaluation reports are likely to be 'flash'.

Oh, I forgot to mention. Evaluation will also be 'goal free', unfettered by notions of programme goals, which will be kept from evaluators like state secrets. The Americans have this on no less an authority than Michael. The British will shake their heads in wonder. So Lawrie was right after all.

Editorial note
The nineteen references to this article are not given. They may be guessed at – and there are no prizes for correct solutions – or they may be obtained through the Editors.

Section 3: Curriculum Research

Introduction

PHILIP H. TAYLOR
University of Birmingham

The first paper presented in this Section, *What is Curriculum Research?*, sparked off a lively debate among the Section membership, a debate which ranged across the many issues which curriculum change, innovation, evaluation and planning raise and how research might help toward the understanding of them as processes which engage the energies of teachers, administrators and scholars. There was strong emphasis placed both on the need to study curriculum phenomena holistically, as all-of-a-piece in their natural setting, and on the need for careful qualitative analysis of the phenomena under research.

This wide ranging discussion was given focus in the presentation of the second paper, *Curriculum Research: A Case Study and some Reflections on Methodology*, and led to the beginnings of an assessment of what research was needed, an assessment which occupied the final session, and resulted in a rough shopping list of some twelve areas for research:

1 Research into why teachers select what they teach and the methods they choose for handling it in the classroom.

2 Studies of the policies which govern curriculum decisions.

3 Research which acts as a monitoring procedure, helping to keep teachers and others informed of effects and changes in the implementation of curricula.

4 Research which leads to a greater awareness of the complexities which surround the institutional settings in which the curriculum is transacted.

5 Research which aims to contribute to a practically useful procedure for curriculum development.

6 Studies of the nature of curriculum decision-making processes.

7 Research concerned to explore the relationship between curricula and the physical conditions of their operation.

8 Studies of the nature and phasing of the child's curriculum, its content and impact.

9 Research which employs concepts from the sociology of knowledge and the sociology of culture.

10 Studies of the influences and constraints which are brought to bear on what is taught in educational institutions.

11 Evaluation studies.

12 Studies of the differential effects of curricula on pupils of different sex, aptitude, home background and personality.

Such a shopping list was by no means exhaustive, as the membership of the Section made plain, nor were they equally agreed on the priority to be given to the items in the list, though they were agreed about, and anxious to foster, a wide ranging research attack on curricular issues.

What is Curriculum Research?

W. A. REID
University of Birmingham

In speaking of curriculum research, I intend to use the word curriculum to refer to a field of study. This usage is less familiar to educators in this country than to their counterparts in the USA, where 'curriculum' has for some time been recognized as an academic 'field' if not an academic discipline (Seguel 1966). By 'curriculum research', therefore, I shall mean 'that research which pertains to the field of Curriculum.' The relationship of such research to educational research as a whole is close, and many of the generalizations which could be applied to the one are also relevant to the other.

Within the more general perspective, it is possible to trace two major and competing traditions. On the one hand there have been those who have studied education and researched into education from a firm base in an established academic discipline. Before the present century they were usually philosophers, often eminent ones such as Locke and Kant. In the early part of this century the philosophers were joined by the psychologists who soon established a dominant position in the academic study of education. More recently this dominance has been challenged by the social scientists. What all these scholars have in common is that they approach the study of education through the use of empirical or analytical methods derived from the concepts and procedures of an academic discipline.

On the other hand there have been those who have worked from the standpoint of the practitioner. In the last century one might point to works such as *Essays on a Liberal Education*, or *Thring's Theory and Practice of Teaching*. The tradition continues to the present day; though latterly on a somewhat more subdued note. It seems unlikely, for example, that we shall see again volumes with such flamboyant titles as *The Headmaster Speaks*. In general, writers of this latter type have shown only a passing familiarity with the disciplines of philosophy, psychology and the social sciences and, far from basing their work on empirical evidence, have often shown a strong aversion to it.

The picture I have painted is a familiar one. On the one hand we have scholars who are apt to be remote from the educational scene, on the other practitioners who are prone to ignore the benefits to be derived from the systematic use of data. But there have always been those who have sought to occupy the middle ground; to take educational problems as their starting point but to be prepared to use whatever support can be gained from empirical and analytical techniques to obtain the results they need. An early example was the work of J. M. Rice on the teaching of spelling (Rice 1897). He was able to show that rote learning of spelling did not produce the results claimed for it, and put into question commonly accepted notions of effective teaching. Workers like Rice would probably have called their field 'pedagogy' or 'instruction'. Neither of these terms has, however, proved attractive to educators in recent years. (Not, at least, in England and the USA, though 'pedagogy' still has currency on the Continent.) The attempt to widen the field under the title of 'Curriculum' was made by Bobbitt, whose book, called quite simply *The Curriculum*, was published in 1918. His concern was to apply systematic techniques to course construction and evaluation, and this has remained the central interest of curriculum studies to the present day (Seguel, pp. 67–90). But increasingly the field has tended to become more complex so that now those who claim their interest as 'Curriculum' point to the fact that, for example, the institutional context within which a curriculum is taught has to be considered as an element which is inseparable from the planning, teaching and evaluation of that curriculum. Westbury and Steimer in a recent article in the *School Review* say, 'We hold that curriculum is a methodical enquiry exploring the range of ways in which the subject matter elements of teacher, student, subject and milieu can be seen' (Westbury and Steimer 1971). Of course, instead of saying 'We hold that curriculum is . . .', they should, perhaps, prefer 'We hold that curriculum *should be* . . .', for some would argue that its concern is with sets of plans or intentions for courses, and that it can encompass nothing more. Recent experience in curriculum development suggests, however, that this is not a particularly useful view to take, and that *all* the problems arising in implementation, whether relating to student, to teacher or to context, need to be taken into account as part of the notion of Curriculum. This is the opinion I would hold, and which I shall have in mind in later sections of this paper.

What I hope to have achieved by introducing an historical perspective, is first of all to have demonstrated that ideas about curriculum as a field of study have grown and evolved over a long period of time, and secondly that the ways in which they have evolved have been due more to a stance adopted towards practical problems, than to the refinement of a concept. Students of curriculum have generally been occupiers of the middle ground to which I referred earlier. Precisely because of this, the problems to which they have addressed themselves have been those relating to the current preoccupations of schools and school systems. As these needs have changed, so have definitions of the field.

To conclude this discussion of curriculum as a field of study, let me present a further definition given by Walker (1973):

> The phenomena of curriculum include all those activities and enterprises in which curricula are planned, created, adopted, presented, experienced, criticized, attacked, defended, and evaluated, as well as the objects which may be part of a curriculum, such as textbooks, apparatus and equipment, schedules, teachers' guides, and so on.
>
> In addition to these actual objects, events and processes, the phenomena of curriculum can be, and in my judgment should be, interpreted to include the plans, intentions, hopes, fears, dreams and the like of agents, such as teachers, students and curriculum developers or policy-makers.

Given that curriculum is a ramified field, and that it is oriented towards the practical concerns of schools and of teachers, how should we understand the term 'curriculum research'? A first step is to point to the distinction which needs to be made between curriculum research and curriculum development. The latter is concerned with the planning, implementation and diffusion of new curricula or new curriculum elements. Examples would be Nuffield Science or Language Projects, the Schools Mathematics Project or the Schools Council Humanities Project. Curriculum developers are *engaged* in the field. Their position is somewhat analogous to that of the engineer, the architect or the sales manager. They do not ignore the results of research; they may, to some extent, carry out research, but it is not their central activity. They are interested in production, administration and publicity. In short, in getting things done. Research, on the other hand, is a process of inquiry, which uses the planned collection and analysis of data to increase understanding of what happens and why. It may help a particular curriculum project or it may not. It may show that the Project was misconceived, which, of course, is not welcome news to someone already embarked on an enterprise which he wants to bring to a successful conclusion. However, the boundary around research cannot be drawn any more tightly than the one around development. Research will be inspired by the experience of development projects, by the need to set up others, and, in its execution, will inevitably be coloured by views about what kinds of curriculum development are useful. Perhaps it is more appropriate to see 'research' and 'development' as opposite poles of a single continuum, in which case many, if not most of those active in the field, would be located somewhere between the two and have an interest in both.

Next the nature of the phenomena which are to be the objects of research needs to be studied. Are they concrete or abstract? Natural or artificial? Living or inert? Are they subject to changing estimations of value or worth? The salient feature of curricula is that they are man-made, and therefore, artificial. The term was used by H. A. Simon in *The Sciences of the Artificial* (1969). Any extended treatment of the nature of curriculum research would demand close reference to his analysis of the nature of social phenomena. It would, therefore, be quite wrong to try to force curriculum research into the traditional paradigms of experimental science which call for clearly defined variables, hypotheses about relationships between them and the applications of tests of significance to test them, other variables being excluded or held constant. (I pass over the fact that the efficacy of this model even for experimental science has recently been questioned by Medawar [1967] and others.) Recent trends in techniques of curriculum evaluation show increasingly the unease which is felt when the experimental model is applied to human situations. This is a good example to take, because most of the research effort in curriculum has, until now, been directed to this kind of activity. At one time there was a reasonable satisfaction with the evaluative model which relied on pretest, post test and control group. Now, however, more intuitive approaches are gaining ground. It has been realized that simple cognitive, or even attitudinal gain models fail to take account many of the considerations which teachers, students and administrators think important in evaluating new curricula. It has also been realized that new curricula imply new aims and that to compare two treatments is not meaningful if the aims envisaged for the two groups are different. Yet another complication arises from the difficulty of specifying the extent to which innovation was, in fact, adopted.

A more recent and more complex model for curriculum evaluation (Stake 1967) will serve very well as a peg on which to hang a wider discussion of the scope of curriculum research. (See Figure 1). This paradigm draws attention to a number of essential features of the process of curriculum evaluation. Most important it makes explicit the fact that in evaluating curricula we are dealing with a dual system. On the left of the diagram we have INTENTS, and on the right, OBSERVATIONS. This exemplifies a dichotomy that runs

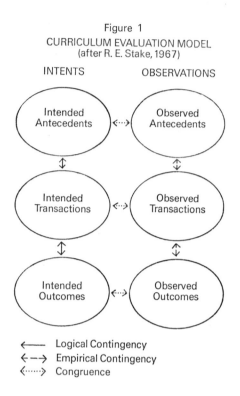

Figure 1
CURRICULUM EVALUATION MODEL
(after R. E. Stake, 1967)

INTENTS   OBSERVATIONS

⟵——— Logical Contingency
⟵ — → Empirical Contingency
⟨······⟩ Congruence

through the whole range of curriculum studies. We are concerned both with what *is* and with what *might be* – with description and with prescription : and both areas should be the subject of research, for what people feel to be important has a strong bearing on what it is possible to bring about. The model also draws attention to the dynamic aspects of the evaluation process. Questions about the outcomes of curricula should, ideally, be related not only to the teaching of the curriculum in the classroom (transactions), but also to what Stake calls 'entering behaviours' of students and teachers – what they already know or believe or are capable of (antecedents). Finally the model shows that relationships between the various cells of the model may be of a different order. The relationships between Intended Antecedents and Intended Transactions is a *logical* one; between Observed Antecedents and Transactions an *empirical* one, and between Intended and Observed Antecedents one of *congruence*.

The paradigm can be readily adapted to the field of curriculum

94

research, and the cells used to generate a variety of possible centres of interest. What aims, intentions and expectations do people have about the curriculum (intended antecedents)? How do they *in fact* set about formulating and describing their intentions and translating them into syllabuses, courses and curriculum materials (observed antecedents)? We have many books and articles to tell us how we ought to plan curricula, but relatively little research to tell us whether these prescriptions bear any relationship to the ways in which people find it necessary to proceed when the task is in front of them. The work of Walker is suggestive of what might be accomplished and, if supported by other researches, would have far-reaching consequences for the choice of strategies of curriculum development (Walker 1971).

Secondly, what kinds of teaching are thought to be effective (intended transactions)? What curriculum content and what teaching methods are actually implemented in schools (observed transactions)? This is another area in which information is lacking. Before attempting to introduce new curricula it would seem necessary to be aware of what is being currently taught. But, as Schwab points out in his article *The Practical – a Language for Curriculum*, our knowledge of this is very deficient (Schwab 1969). Programmes and statements of aims are readily available, but the extent to which programmes are implemented, or aims translated into activities is uncertain. Here again some pointers are available to the kinds of researches which might be attempted. An illustrative example is to be found in the work of Hodgetts, whose simply conceived but powerfully illuminative survey of what happens in the Canadian Studies Classroom raises fundamental questions about the curriculum as teachers and pupils experience it (Hodgetts 1972).

Thirdly, what kinds of outcomes do we expect from our curricula, and what outcomes do we actually get (intended and observed outcomes)? These are questions which have been salient in work on evaluation and have received a good deal of attention. It is still far from certain, however, that we have found adequate ways of treating them, though as Professor Eggleston's paper which follows shows, encouraging progress is being made.

However, as I emphasized earlier, I would think it necessary in pursuing research to go on beyond questions which are internal to the curriculum and to look also at how the curriculum relates to institutions and to society generally. In what ways does the curriculum respond to institutional, social and political constraints? How does the curriculum of the school reflect ideas which are held in society about what is desirable knowledge and who should possess it? To see curricula merely as phenomena of schooling misses the vital point that they are a social fact having necessary relationships with social forces outside the school.

This is an area of research which is rapidly gaining recognition, though in a variety of guises. Taylor (1973) has characterized it as a 'new frontier', and workers such as Young (1971) in this country and Kirst and Walker (1971) in the USA have in their different ways and from different standpoints helped to give it a strong impetus.

These observations about the questions to which research might address itself have implications for the methodologies which might be adopted. Many of the kinds of research which I have mentioned must depend, partly at least, on a case study approach. In fields which are in a constant state of flux, where the chance of finding enduring relationships is minimal, and where the number of variables to be controlled is almost infinite, there is little gain and much to lose from a heavy investment in geographically extensive sample surveys. Since we cannot filter the uniqueness out of any educational situation we are, as researchers, better advised to accept the inevitability of ambiguity, and to aim for impressionistic data, for insights, for clarifications, for ways of looking at things, rather than for theorems, laws, constants and calculuses. Complex data, if they are to mean anything, must have a unity, and a natural unity is imparted by studying groups, classes, schools and local districts. It is also imparted by the single observer, or team of observers, who can modify and amplify their research plan as they go along. Seldom is it possible to do this with the single extensive sample survey.

Even where the case study is not the answer to a particular problem, some kind of limited case work is almost certainly desirable before wider enquiries are attempted. Without a preliminary effort of this kind it is almost impossible to sort out the questions which should be asked from the almost infinite number which might be asked. Once questions have been identified techniques of investigation can be chosen to suit them. These may stem from psychology, sociology, organizational analysis or a variety of other sources. What matters is that the source is chosen to suit the question and not vice versa.

Turning finally to techniques of data analysis, we must have regard to the fact that curriculum researchers are occupying the middle ground which I mentioned before. They are therefore, implicitly or explicitly, claiming to produce results of practical relevance to the planners, developers, implementors and evaluators of curricula. If they are to do this successfully, the methods of statistical analysis they employ must be capable of leading to conclusions which are readily understandable. Simple procedures may be preferred to those which are logically and mathematically elegant, but which seem to practical people to give results which are devoid of meaning. To research into a practical field is not to accept only the handicap of a clientele unattuned to sophisticated measures. On the positive side, the viability of analytical procedures can often be checked against the practical experience of those engaged in the field. It may be, for instance, that a technique such as factor analysis, producing results which have to be impressionistically interpreted, will yield conclusions which teachers and others recognize as appropriate characterizations of educational phenomena. For example the group of primary school teachers which discussed the findings of some research recently carried out from the Birmingham Teaching Research Unit were able to recognize the dimensions of their own experience in factor analyses of the constraints which teachers felt themselves to work under and the influences to which they were subjected in planning and implementing the curriculum (Taylor, Reid, Holley and Exon in press).

If I am right in my contention that the tradition of curriculum research stems from a desire to occupy a middle ground between studies of education which are based on academic disciplines and studies growing out of personal experiences and feelings, then, as I have said, its justification must be sought in the fact that it can provide the kinds of data which policy makers find relevant to their tasks. This may mean leaning in the direction of rather straightforward, simplistic approaches to research problems, for we have not yet reached a stage at which our policy making processes are capable of absorbing complex and refined data. If research is conducted in a purely academic spirit then its inability to affect policy will not worry us. My own feeling is that those who have a commitment to curriculum research would not be happy with such a state of affairs.

We must also look to the fact that the processes by which curricula are determined at any level are in many respects political. Though the written curriculum may seem to relate purely to the communication of knowledge, the processes leading to the promulgation of a written curriculum and the processes whereby it is translated into classroom activities involve adjustments and accommodations between human beings, the definition of issues, the establishing of priorities and the allocation of scarce resources.

The constraints put upon curriculum research by the nature of the data it has to handle and the kinds of decision processes to which its results relate, both seem at the present moment to tend in the same direction – towards a naturalistic, humanistic, impressionistic mode of research, with an emphasis on description, on case study, and on a stance which recognizes the political nature of much curriculum activity.

This is not an easy position to accept. Many people, especially those holding administrative positions, are not well disposed to research which is impressionistic in nature. They like to have certainty. To this must be added the fact that the 'scientific' model of research has achieved a high level of academic and even popular respectability and it is not easy for research workers to abandon it. Nevertheless, we may conclude it is better to do so if we seriously wish to confront the issues central to the activity of curriculum research.

References

BOBBIT, F. (1918) *The Curriculum* Boston: Houghton Mifflin

HODGETTS, A. B. (1972) *What Culture? What Heritage? A Study of Civic Education in Canada* Toronto: OISE

KIRST, M. W. and WALKER, D. F. (1971) An Analysis of Curriculum Policy-Making *Review of Educational Research* 41, 5, 479–509

MEDAWAR, P. B. (1967) *The Art of the Soluble* London: Methuen

RICE, J. (1897) The Futility of the Spelling Grind *Forum* 23, 163–72

SCHWAB, J. J. (1969) The Practical: a Language for Curriculum *School Review* 78, 1, 1–23

SEGUEL, M. L. (1966) *The Curriculum Field: its Formative Years* New York: Teachers College Press

SIMON, H. A. (1969) *The Sciences of the Artificial* Cambridge, Mass.: MIT Press

STAKE, R. E. (1967) The Countenance of Curriculum Evaluation *Teachers College Record* 68, 523–40

TAYLOR, P. H. (1973) New Frontiers in Educational Research, *Paedogogica Europaea*

TAYLOR, P. H., REID, W. A., HOLLEY, B. J. and EXON, G. (in press) *Purpose, Power and Constraint in the Primary School Curriculum* London: Macmillan for the Schools Council

WALKER, D. F. (1971) A Naturalistic Model for Curriculum Development *School Review* 80, 1, 56–65

WALKER, D. F. (1973) What Curriculum Research? *Journal of Curriculum Studies* 5, 1

WESTBURY, I., and STEIMER, W. (1971) Curriculum: a Discipline in Search of its Problems *School Review* 79, 2, 243–68

YOUNG, M. F. D. (Ed) (1971) *Knowledge and Control* London: Collier-Macmillan

Curriculum Research: A Case Study and some Reflections on Methodology

J. F. EGGLESTON
University of Nottingham

Introduction

By the time the Schools Council Project for the Evaluation of Science Teaching Methods got into the evaluation business, Nuffield O level biology, chemistry and physics teams had packed their bags. They left behind their respective curriculum packages and tailor-made O levels. The time for *formative* evaluation had passed. Had the dawn of *summative* evaluation come?

Lee Cronbach had told us nearly ten years ago that evaluation is 'the collection and use of information to make decisions about an educational programme'; 'that the greatest service evaluation can perform is to identify aspects of a course which need revision'; that 'the aim to compare one course with another should not dominate plans for evaluation.' He saw evaluation at its most effective when in its formative role, 'while (the course) is still fluid.' Cronbach's proposed style of evaluation included the opinion of scholars about the course; the soliciting of reports from teachers on pupils' accomplishments, reactions and attitudes, as well as more objective, public and generalizable evidence of 'systematic observation' including process studies, cognitive and attitudinal measures (Cronbach 1963).

The three Nuffield O level science projects seem to have followed Cronbach's prescription at least part of the way. It is doubtful that any curriculum development in science achieved Cronbach's ambition to determine 'the post-course performance of a well-described group, with respect to many important objectives and side effects', at least in a manner which facilitates an adequate description. It is even less certain that the evaluators conceived their task as Cronbach described it, 'to understand how the course produces its effects and what parameters influenced its effectiveness.'

I do not doubt that faced with some evidence of achievement or lack of achievement, or some manifestation of enthusiasm or boredom, evaluators speculated on causal links between pupils' experience and achievement. Indeed, the collection of evidence subsequent to the production of the final version of the materials has been accompanied by a good deal of informed speculation on causes, particularly causes of failure to comprehend parts of the course. Nevertheless, the establishment of causal links between 'course parameters' and outcomes may be not only secondary in the mind of the evaluator but impossible to achieve anyway, given the constraints with which he normally has to work.

One-shot case studies

Scriven (1967) labelled this kind of evaluation *formative* and pointed to the need for comparative studies on a post-development *summative* evaluation. The demonstration of the need for comparative studies rests on tenets that are fundamental to a scientific demonstration of cause and effect. As Campbell and Stanley (1963) assert, 'basic to scientific evidence (and to all knowledge-diagnostic process including the retina of the eye) is the process of comparison, or recording differences, or of contrast'. These authors reject what they call one-shot case studies, i.e. a design in which a single group is studied only once subsequent to exposure to some agent or treatment presumed to cause change. Such studies, they say, 'have such a total absence of control as to be of almost no scientific value.' Pupils may be exposed to an experimental treatment such as a curriculum 'package' and their behaviour, including that taken as evidence of achievement, may be observed. A design which lacks comparison fails to equip the investigator with the information he needs in order to determine how much, if any, of the variation in observed behaviour was due to the treatment.

In practice, although it may offend fundamental canons of scientific methodology, much formative evaluation is of this one-shot case study kind. Attempts have been made to improve matters by measuring *growth* rather than final state only, that is differences in behaviour before and after exposure to 'treatment'. Now the effects on the variation of growth due to factors not controlled by the experimenter may be specified but cannot be measured. These include history, (events uncontrolled or even unknown by the experimenter); maturation; the effect of testing; errors of instrumentation, possible Hawthorn effects and others.

One-shot case studies in evaluation are illustrated in Figures 1 and 2 opposite.

Many evaluators would, within limits, testify to the usefulness of such designs as those illustrated. Cronbach would agree with them. There seems to be a flat contradiction between Campbell and Stanley's description of the shortcomings of one-shot case studies and their proven usefulness in evaluation practice. At first sight this may seem a puzzling dilemma, but it is not difficult to imagine how

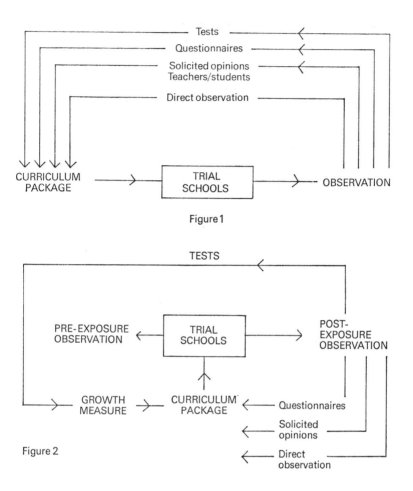

Figure 1

Figure 2

certain observed effects, such as pupil behaviour after a single exposure to 'treatment', might inform curriculum developers that the 'treatment' requires modification. Particular examples might be the class experiment which fails in trial schools to give consistent results, or a chunk of text which is more often than not met with blank incomprehension. These then are observed effects which would cause curriculum developers to act. In these two cases it is not easy to see how controls could be set up or how they would help if they were.

A feature common to both these examples is that they are concerned with means rather than ends. Whatever objective one might hope to achieve by the successful completion of the experiment, pupils will fail to achieve it if the experiment fails to give consistent predictable results. It is of course impossible to be certain on this point without knowing the objectives and the context in which the experiment occurred. Nevertheless, circumstances might conspire to produce a situation in which a reliable result was necessary to advance some enquiry in the course of which some objectives might be achieved. On the other hand, it may be that some teachers ignore the bit of text following the experiment and capitalize on the experiment's failure to enquire further into possible causes of this unpredictability of results. The curriculum developer is then faced with a decision to abandon the experiment, or to leave it in the course but rewrite the text. This example goes some way towards resolving the dilemma. There seems to be a fairly clear-cut distinction between those observations which inform us about *means* and those concerned with *ends*. When experiments fail to give consistent results and when a key paragraph in a text is found to be incomprehensible, some obviously necessary conditions for the achievement of any desirable outcome are lacking. A sub-set of observed effects may thus inform curriculum developers that components in a curriculum package are not operating as intended. It is inherent in the process of developing curriculum packages that the authors have certain expectations about the behaviour of pupils and teachers and that they make assumptions about the properties of the materials in the packages they produce. These expectations and assumptions constitute a pre-specification of the treatment variables. One-shot case studies may function effectively when they inform the curriculum developer that the minimal conditions exist which facilitate the operation of specified treatment variables. Indeed, it might be profitable to redefine the term *formative evaluation* to include only those observations which yield this information.

However, when we know that the necessary minimal conditions for the package to function exist and measured outcomes exhibit variation, what we cannot do, as Campbell and Stanley argue, is to determine the proportion of the variance in outcomes due to treatment and that proportion due to such factors as testing effects, maturation, and the like.

Experimental designs
Scriven follows Campbell and Stanley in affirming that in order to relate cause to effect we require at best a true experimental design (Scriven 1967). Such a design minimizes the risk of invalidity and facilitates the apportionment of variance due to treatment. This may be translated into a design for summative evaluation of a curriculum package as follows in Figure 3.

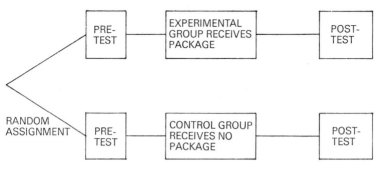

Figure 3

An attempt at a true experimental approach to summative evaluation would consist of the following steps:

1 From a 'population' of target schools (usually classes within schools and their teachers) select two samples at random.
2 Produce a large resource of 'test' items covering a wide range of cognitive and attitudinal variables which include those related to the objectives of the curriculum package under test as well as other *anticipated* outcomes. (Note that it is impossible to pre-test outcomes that are not anticipated!)
3 Pre-test both samples (or random sub-sets from each sample) on selected variables.
4 Assign one random sample to the curriculum package treatment and the 'equalized group' to no package.
5 Post-test both groups and compare class means (or random subset means) from the two samples.

Cronbach, and more recently Parlett (Parlett and Hamilton 1972), reject this approach to evaluation on the grounds that where 'formally designed experiments pitting one course against another' have been carried out on measured variables, the results 'are rarely definitive enough to justify their cost.' Cronbach goes on to say, 'differences between average test scores resulting from different courses are usually small, relative to the wide differences among and within classes taking the same course.' Parlett's grounds for rejection include cost of time and resources; and the arguments that 'strict control is rarely followed', and that the simulation of 'laboratory conditions by "manipulating educational personnel" is ... dubious ethically.' Stephens (1967) too, after reviewing experiments on instruction over a 50-year period noted 'a remarkable constancy of educational results in the face of widely differing educational approaches'. These authors are unanimous at least in rejecting this design because it fails to demonstrate different results from different treatments.

Noting the exception of the improved 'performance of students in studies of good programmed texts,' Scriven accepts the above observation. He says, 'initially one's tendency is to feel that the mountain has laboured and brought forth a mouse,' but does not accept Cronbach's conclusion. He points out that providing (and this is a major proviso) that the test instruments are adequate to their task, and given that the design is not confounded by some methodological artefact, it is 'extremely informative to discover parity of performance'. If Scriven observes no difference he is prepared to accept that there may be no difference.

Cronbach's second line of attack on experimental studies is methodological. He points to the analogy of trials on a new therapeutic drug and the use of a double blind in such trials. Here all the pills look the same. Neither the doctors administering the drug nor the patients know which pills contain the drug and which pills are placebos. Doctors and patients are actively involved in trying to improve the patients' health and if they knew which pill contained the drug their behaviour would become a potentially important factor (independent variable) in bringing about an improvement in the patients' condition (dependent variable). If the analogue of the pill is the curriculum package, the analogue of the doctor is the teacher, that of the patient, the student. There can be no placebo. The teacher (and probably the students) will know that they are being 'treated' to a curriculum package.

Scriven's recipe for a solution to this problem is forthright. 'First, we get two graduate students or instructors in (let us suppose) economics, given them a vocabulary list for the tenth grade and pay them $500 a chapter for a translation of Samuelson's text into tenth-grade language, encouraging them to use their originality in introducing new ideas. They could probably handle the whole text in a summer and so for a few thousand dollars, including costs of reproducing pilot materials, we have something we could set up against one of the fancier economics curricula based on a great deal of high-priced help and laborious field-testing. Then we find a couple of really bright college juniors, majoring in economics, from different colleges, and give *them* a summer to turn their recent experience at the receiving end of introductory economics courses, and their current acquaintance with the problems of concept grasping in the field, into a curriculum outline . . .' etc!

To British, if not American readers, such a recipe has a Beetonian ring about it, but this is Scriven's placebo, or, more accurately, multiple placebo. Comparisons are now possible between alternative curriculum packages where effects due to 'enthusiasm' and related Hawthorn effects are hopefully matched across groups. So far as we know no one has shown the courage of Scriven's convictions. Scriven's design is illustrated in Figure 4.

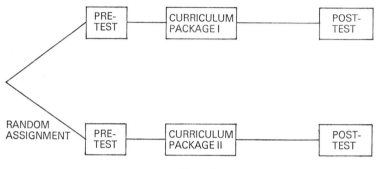

Figure 4

It is still true that, where comparisons have been made under conditions which approach those described in Figure 4, differences are small or insignificant (statistically speaking). Now, Scriven must be right to conclude that if no deficiency can be found in either the measuring instruments used or the design of the study, then, no observed difference means that there is no difference. However, both Cronbach and Scriven seem less than happy with the range, specificity, sensitivity and accuracy of existing measuring instruments. Although we share this concern, our efforts have been employed in exploring an aspect of the methodology illustrated in Figure 4.

Teachers-pupils-curriculum packages as interacting systems
The fact that evaluations based on this comparative, experimental design have rarely demonstrated statistically significant differences in the selected outcomes, must lead to the conclusion that whatever differentiated the experimental group from the control group often failed to produce a consistent measurable difference in attainment between the groups. Such findings have led some researchers in this field, who find such an assault on their primary assumptions about the conditions for learning untenable, to reject the 'methods of the agronomist' (pejorative term) and search for alternative methodologies for evaluation. The complexity of the learning environment and its many related and often unknown variables has led some researchers to such disciplines as social anthropology for the conceptual and methodological models they require to investigate

the effects of a curriculum package. Before recommending such an extreme course, it is profitable to re-examine some features of the 'experimental' model for defects which may not be due to inherent faults but to the particular application of the model to the evaluation of curriculum packages.

The design illustrated in Figure 4 merits further consideration, not only to effect the kind of improvement suggested by Scriven but also critically to examine one of its built-in assumptions. The single consistent difference between the experimental group and the control group is either that one receives a curriculum package and the other does not, or that one receives the curriculum package and the other an alternative package. The conditions which together are necessary and sufficient to establish a statistically significant difference between the groups in any measure of attainment are, that the variation of the class scores within a group, with respect to the group mean, is less than the variation of all classes, with respect to the mean of all classes, in both groups; and that the group means differ by a large enough amount.

It is helpful to think of causes of differences between class mean scores as making a contribution to variation (variance) of these scores, and then to partition this variance between causes and according to the relative strengths of their effects. Thus if we could identify all the causes of variance between means we would account for all (100%) of the variance.

Now one of the necessary conditions for *any given cause* to be established empirically is that it accounts for more than say, 5% of the variance. It may be that in all those cases where the curriculum package produced no significant difference it accounted for less than 5% of the variance of the class mean scores. In other words, the failure to demonstrate significant differences between the two groups on some measured outcome, may be due to the far greater contribution to the variation of scores of causes other than the use of a curriculum package. It is precisely these potential causes of variance which the scheme shown in Figure 4 by random assignment 'equalized' across the groups.

Because a curriculum package is frequently designed, written, and then implemented on a trials basis by teachers, it is reasonable to assume that some teachers, before the curriculum development was conceived, embraced some of the curriculum development team's objectives and taught in a manner designed to achieve these objectives. It is possible that some teachers out-Nuffielded Nuffield. Where random assignment is used to select two groups, experimental and control, such a teacher is as likely to be picked for either group. Thus in the experimental group there may be teachers who by their tactical decisions – by their teaching style – augment the materials; and others who could by their style negate any influence the package might have. The same applies to the control group. It follows that because teachers mediate between the curriculum package and the pupils, it might be more profitable initially to explore those components of the learning environment which play a part in determining how the materials are used. What this means, in effect, is that an important first step in summative evaluation is to determine how far the treatment to which any randomly selected group is exposed has any claim to equivalence.

The adequate specification of the treatment variable
There is probably enough evidence available to suggest that except in the case of proven 'teacher-proof' materials, curriculum packages should never be considered alone as a major independent variable. We are back to the problem of specifying the treatment variable. Presumably an effective formative evaluation will have identified the more obvious effects of extraneous variables on the operation of the curriculum package. Now we are faced with variables which must interact with the package to give rise to a whole set of interactions. If, for example, 'extraneous' variables were identified in teachers' behaviour, the interaction between package and teacher might in the extreme case result in as many different versions of the package as there are teachers using it. Our problem now is to identify sources of variation in the treatment which may interact with the curriculum package and determine the observed effects. It is at this point that an established theory of learning would help. In the absence of such a theory a body of experience organized into perceptual schema in the minds of teachers and researchers is helpful.

When interest centres round a particular product of an educational system, related schema may yield potentially rich sources of variation which may set limits on the effectiveness of a curriculum package. One such schema which is clearly shared by many evaluators is that of teacher-pupil-resources interaction. Many schema, and this is no exception, tend to be derived from a large data base. One problem facing the evaluator is to reduce this data base to manageable proportions by a search for major components of the schema which together constitute the dimensions of a tidy conceptual model. Such a model can become a way of organizing descriptions of events which attend the use of a curriculum package. The process might be visualized as shown on page 108.

The two tracks round this diagram indicate in general terms two ways of procuring useful data. Track B is favoured by the *illuminative* evaluators (see Parlett and Hamilton 1972), where, for example, a social anthropologist observes the context of learning and, using his 'model', attends to those events relevant to it, interpreting the events in terms of the dynamics of his model. Track A is an empirical track. A general schema is used to identify relevant variables which are observed. Later, by some form of correlational analysis, these variables are reduced to a small number of factors which together account for variation in the data. In this way, measures which relate to components or factors in the model may be investigated to determine their possible links with the achievement of objectives by correlational studies. They may later be used to test the causal nature of these links by experimental studies, either independent of, or when interacting with, a curriculum package.

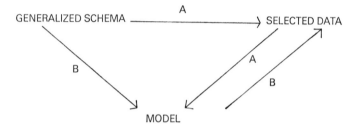

Part of the work of the Research Unit for the Evaluation of Science Teaching Methods has been to attempt to derive such a model from the general schema in teacher-pupil-resources-interaction as it relates to the intellectual transactions between teachers and pupils, among pupils, and between pupils and resources. Ninety-six science teachers teaching pupils of comparable ability were observed on three occasions. Observations were made in 23 categories of teacher and pupil cognitive behaviour, such as the kinds of questions they ask, the kinds of statements they make, and directions they give. By recording a tally mark when a teacher or pupils behaved in one of these 23 particular ways within predetermined time intervals, it was possible to translate the lessons into a descriptive profile of intellectual transactions. A range of variation between teachers was thus observed and described. For example, seven different kinds of teacher's questions were recorded. These were designated as: Teacher asks questions (or invites comments) which are answered by:

a_1 recalling facts and principles
a_2 applying facts and principles to problem solving
a_3 making hypothesis or speculation

a_4 designing of experimental procedure
a_5 direct observation
a_6 interpretation of observed or recorded data
a_7 making inferences from observations or data

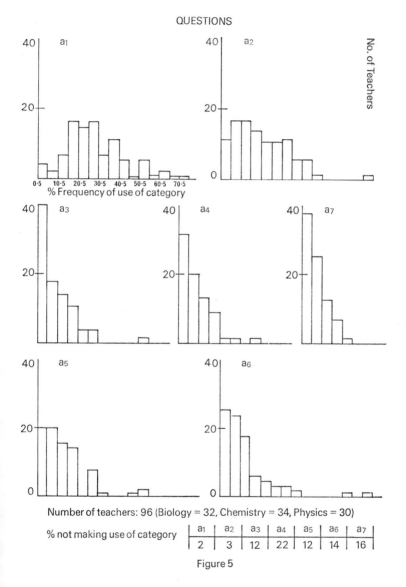

Figure 5

The frequencies of use of these categories by different teachers are illustrated as histograms in Figure 5. These data show a large variation between teachers within some categories, particularly in categories a_1 and a_2, and considerable differences of frequency of use between categories.

Data were available for all 23 categories for all 96 teachers. It was then possible to attempt to sort teachers and their classes and to find out if there were groups within which there was a constancy of what might be called cognitive style, the essential components of which could be identified. Within each group, variation in these components would ideally be small, while differences between groups in these components would be large. The problem was that of determining which, if any, of the 23 behaviours go together and then deciding if the associated categories constitute a pedagogical significant style. The application of *cluster analysis*, (a procedure designed for the purpose of grouping objects or phenomena according to similarities of observed properties), to the data suggested that a tentative sorting of these teachers and their classes into three groups was possible. In order to make the 'thumb nail' sketches of each of these three groups intelligible, the 23 categories of the *Science Teaching Observation Schedule* (Eggleston, Galton and Jones, in press) used in this research is given as an appendix to this paper.

The picture which emerged of the first group of teachers/classes is one in which the initiative is held by the teacher, who challenges his pupils with a comprehensive range of questions – factual, inferential and speculative – in both theoretical and practical contexts. It is probable that teacher demonstration predominates over class practical work. The major distinguishing feature of the group is the incidence of problem-solving activity. (The definition of problem solving used in this research was restricted by giving this activity a somewhat convergent character.) It is this kind of activity in which these teachers/classes relatively frequently engage. Pupil-initiated and maintained activity tends to run at a relatively low level except where it is related to problem solving.

The second group of teachers/classes was in many respects quite different from the first and the third groups. Thus the major distinguishing feature is the use of categories concerned with facts and principles. Teachers' statements tended predominantly to be of this kind, and so did the questions they asked and the directions they gave. Even when initiative passed into the hands of the pupils, they too sought or consulted or referred to teacher for the purpose of acquiring or confirming facts and principles. Those categories of behaviour concerned with speculation, experimental work and those of an inferential character distinguish this group in a negative sense. They were relatively little in evidence.

The unique features of the third group all fall in the major divisions under 'Talk and activity initiated and/or maintained by pupils.' Pupils sought information or consulted for the purpose of making inferences, formulating or testing hypotheses; pupils referred to teacher for the purpose of seeking guidance when making inferences, formulating or testing hypotheses; and when seeking guidance on experimental procedure. In other respects this group tended to resemble both the other groups, but its teachers were less likely to make factual statements and more likely to ask questions of interpretation than teachers in the second group. The general picture one got of this group was, broadly speaking, consistent with pupil-directed enquiry.

If subsequent analysis confirms these first tentative groupings the implications for the implementation of new curriculum developments in science are clear. To know the patterns of teacher-pupil interaction in classes which will receive a curriculum package which is to be empirically tested, is to have the means for measuring interaction effects which would otherwise sink without trace.

It is particularly important to know, at the formative evaluation stage, if the style of teacher-pupil interaction is in some cases incompatible with the package; to know if the experience enjoyed by the pupils exposed to the package is as the authors intended it to be; to know that the treatment variables are operating as specified.

When a teacher/class receives a curriculum package it may be that the pattern of their interaction changes, a trend which may be accentuated as the package is 'recycled' with subsequent classes. Pupil-teacher interaction may thus profitably be regarded as a major dependent variable in the formative stages of a curriculum development.

Summary and conclusions
1 Formative evaluation, when it is a one-shot case study (methodologically speaking), can inform us only that the treatment variable is operating as intended. It cannot result in proven causal explanations of success or failure.
2 True experimental studies in summative evaluation seem to have been premature, based too often on a curriculum package specification only.
3 These are more potent determinants of achievement which dwarf the variation due to curriculum packages.
4 These other factors which singly, or interacting with each

other or with the curriculum package, may produce visible effects and measurable differences and can probably be identified.

5 A useful first stage of evaluation might be to use teacher-pupil interaction as a dependent variable prior to a second stage where the curriculum package is assigned to teachers/classes, identified according to their interaction style. In this way interactions between 'style' and package may be determined.

Appendix

Science Teaching Observation Schedule

1 TEACHER TALK
1a *Teacher asks questions (or invites comments) which are answered by:*
a_1 recalling facts and principles
a_2 applying facts and principles to problem solving
a_3 making hypothesis or speculation
a_4 designing of experimental procedure
a_5 direct observation
a_6 interpretation of observed or recorded data
a_7 making inferences from observations or data

1b *Teacher makes statements:*
b_1 of facts and principles
b_2 of problems
b_3 of hypothesis or speculation
b_4 of experimental procedure

1c *Teacher directs pupils to sources of information for the purpose of :*
c_1 acquiring or confirming facts or principles
c_2 identifying or solving problems
c_3 making inferences, formulating or testing hypotheses
c_4 seeking guidance on experimental procedure

2 TALK AND ACTIVITY INITIATED AND/OR MAINTAINED BY PUPILS

2d *Pupils seek information or consult for the purpose of:*
d_1 acquiring or confirming facts or principles
d_2 identifying or solving problems
d_3 making inferences, formulating or testing hypotheses

d$_4$ clarifying experimental procedure

2e *Pupils refer to teachers for the purpose of:*
e$_1$ acquiring or confirming facts or principles
e$_2$ seeking guidance when identifying or solving problems
e$_3$ seeking guidance when making inferences, formulating or testing hypotheses
e$_4$ seeking guidance on experimental procedure

References

CAMPBELL, D. T., STANLEY, J. C. (1963) Experimental and Quasi-Experimental Designs for Research on Teaching *Handbook of Research on Teaching* (ed. N. L. GAGE) Chicago: Rand McNally and Co. pp. 171–246

CRONBACH, L. J. (1963) Course Improvement through Evaluation *Teachers College Record*, 64, 8, 672–83

EGGLESTON, J. F., GALTON, M. and JONES, M. (in press) *A Science Teaching Observation Schedule* Schools Council Research Publications

PARLETT, M. and HAMILTON, D. (1972) Evaluation as Illumination: A New Approach to the Study of Innovatory Programmes *Occasional Paper No. 9* Centre for Research into Educational Sciences; University of Edinburgh

SCRIVEN, M. (1967) The Methodology of Evaluation *Perspectives of Curriculum Evaluation* (ed. R. TYLER, R. GAGNE, M. SCRIVEN) *AERA* Monograph Series on Curriculum Evaluation No. 1 Chicago: Rand McNally and Company pp. 39–83

STEPHENS, J. (1967) *The Process of Schooling; a Psychological Examination* New York: Holt, Rinehart and Winston

H

Section 4: The Schools and their Curriculum

Introduction

JACK WALTON
University of Exeter

The authors of both papers in this section attempted to respond to the initial statement given to them prior to the conference:

> The curriculum of schools provides the boundaries of possible learning for its pupils, and the management of schools, their buildings and other resources, together with the teaching which pupils receive, determine what pupils will in fact be asked to learn.

In his contribution Professor Skilbeck identified and clarified some of the curriculum issues arising from the current interest in what is loosely referred to as 'open education' or 'open schooling'. These issues are numerous and diverse and they are difficult to bring into sharp focus in a period of great fluidity and rapid change in education. Nevertheless, when there is so much advocacy of a more 'open' approach to schooling, it is important to consider what is intended by this advocacy and to reflect on its implications, including some of the problems to which it might give rise in curriculum thinking. The approach he adopted was to examine briefly a series of related points on curriculum definition: moves towards a more 'open' approach to curriculum content and organization, criteria governing educational processes, the significance of pupil and teacher standpoints, and ways of structuring curricula to achieve educational and cultural goals. The paper ended with a series of problems in recent curriculum theory which might provide the starting point for further inquiry.

The second paper, accepting both the identification and the clarification proposed by Professor Skilbeck, directed its attention to a consideration in more detail of the restraints faced by the curriculum practitioner and the learner within the school. While both primary and secondary education were considered, perhaps a greater emphasis was given to the secondary field, where the constraints are more apparent and determining. It was suggested that there is a tendency to regard restraints as immutable rather than problematic. Specific attention was given to the arrangement of time and it was suggested that within the institution time is often the independent variable upon which other variables depend. The results of modifying the time factor were suggested and discussed. Particular attention was given to the effect such modification appears to have on the more traditional styles of teaching, types of resources and architectural characteristics.

Openness and Structure in the Curriculum

MALCOLM SKILBECK
New University of Ulster

Rethinking the curriculum for both openness and structure

The theme 'Openness and structure in the curriculum' provides a convenient opportunity for raising some of the interesting problems in curriculum theory which have been the subject of much controversy in recent years. At the same time, we may be able to bring into sharper focus questions of a highly practical nature in which many school people at present are engrossed. I don't wish to imply that a single short paper is the appropriate vehicle for such a wide-ranging analysis of these umbrella-like concepts – 'openness' and 'structure'. However, the task of this particular section of the conference is, presumably, to range widely across the territory which connects reflection to action. Therefore I would like to introduce what I take to be some of the critical issues arising from the attempt to re-think school curricula so as to make them, at one and the same time, both more open and more structured. The paper has been prepared as a discussion document, not as a finished essay, whereby we may make a modest contribution towards understanding and action in one of the more problematic areas of contemporary educational experience.

One of our preliminary difficulties in approaching this problem is a confusing use of language in curriculum discussions. If we start with the broader conception of curriculum which is now in favour, we may find it impossible to discuss open and structured curricula with any degree of precision. Thus, 'open curriculum' will be indistinguishable from 'open schools' and indeed 'open education'. For a start, at any rate, I want to anchor the discussion by proposing that the curriculum be thought of as a chart of learning experiences which is laid out and made available by a school in pursuit of its educational objectives. Learning experiences, in so far as they are a school responsibility, are structured; they are not open in the sense of being indeterminate. Learning experiences, within the curriculum, embody educational values. They are arranged according to more or less definite views about learning processes, about general human development, about the expectations of various groups external to the school, and about what is feasible and desirable in an institutional setting where many constraints limit the realization of the values to which educators aspire. The curriculum, on this view, is distinctive of an institution – the school – or of an institutional-ized process, schooling.

Many factors, both external and internal to the school, enter into and vitally influence the curriculum and affect our efforts to modify it. However, I am not proposing to call these influences 'the curriculum' any more than I would call the weather or the products of the chemical industry 'farming' simply because farming is influenced by factors of rainfall, sunshine, fertilizer and so forth. By 'curriculum' I mean a set of intentional activities, those of educators who, to the extent that they seek to bring about changes in others, i.e. pupils, in a regular, orderly manner, institutionalize these activities. In other words, schooling is the institutional medium of educational expression and curriculum is one of the major activities of schooling.

Education as a structured process

It will be apparent that in my discussion I am proposing to emphasize structure. Rather than admitting a dichotomy between 'structure' and 'openness' which is educationally significant, I will argue that structures may be more or less open, and that educational situations, including curriculum situations, are never completely open. To argue that educational situations can be completely open is to argue that any experience is or can be an educational experience. This argument carries with it the implication that there are no criteria by which we can distinguish educational from other experiences or processes. When we reach this point, we no longer have anything interesting or useful to say about education, and the word itself, like the distinctive experiences of 'being educated', might as well pass out of existence. It may be that some advocates of 'open systems' in education are moving rapidly in this direction. Of course, it does not follow from what I have said that schools exist only for educational purposes, or that the major feature of a school should be its curricula. However, if schools are increasingly going to have to satisfy other than educational criteria, or if they wish to lay greater emphasis on matters other than the curriculum, it is as well to be clear that this is what they are about.

The opening up of educational opportunities

In emphasizing structures, I am not wishing to diminish the value of the world-wide regeneration of educational thinking and systems now taking place. It is one of the features of this movement that the old limitations, the structures which have come to operate as limiting factors and as means of sustaining the privileges, advantages, and power of tiny minorities are collapsing. An 'open' educational system in this context may be thought of as one which widens opportunity: not only opportunity of access but, (and this is very much in the school's hands), opportunity for experience of educational significance within the school. This is not to be equated with opening up opportunity for social mobility, one of the blind alleys into which education has been led by a group of reformers who have concentrated on the short-term policy of mobility upwards and in the material realm. Schools need to recognize that, in our kind of society, upward mobility for some still means downward mobility for others.

Curriculum diversity is essential, and much greater diversity than we are accustomed to, if opportunity for educative experience within the framework of schooling is to become a meaningful option for all pupils. A further point is that while schooling may become less open in the access it provides to 'good' jobs, it is becoming more open in the access it provides to further forms of education: curricula need to be open in the sense of opening up opportunities for continuing personal and social development. The concept of continuing education has radical implications for our ideas about appropriate performance in the secondary schools. School curricula which are not stimulating, sustaining, achievement-orientated and built on the analysis of contemporary culture, are unlikely to provide that platform from which lifelong education and cultural progress proceed. These curricula must free themselves from the dominance of performance criteria which are encapsulated in public examinations. The 'right time' for performance according to public examinations need not be restricted to the present period of schooling.

Making distinctively educational decisions

In proposing that we adopt an educational stance in considering curriculum matters, I am still leaving open the question of what counts as an educational decision. What conditions need to be satisfied if we are to speak confidently about the educative value of our curricula? I think we can proceed by eliminating some of the more attractive claimants – not in the sense of dismissing their importance but in the sense of their being treated as adequate answers to the question – are our curricula educative? These more attractive claimants include 'interest', 'relevance' and 'social need': a curriculum may be interesting and relevant, and satisfy certain social needs and yet not be especially educative. This is because in seeking for educational criteria we cannot be content with the minimum level of want satisfaction which is all that is necessary to meet the requirements of these three criteria. We need no concept at all of education in order to describe a process whereby X satisfies the wants of Y.

In the recent and current discussions of a curriculum appropriate to the mass population of the secondary school, especially the 'early leavers', much has been recommended that does not strike me as educative. It may be countered that the schools have had a problem thrust upon them and that they need to develop procedures for coping with certain difficulties. Schools may, and do, engage in all sorts of things in addition to their educational work. Yet American experience of similar situations after World War II, when 'life adjustment' programmes became very popular as a form of coping behaviour, might usefully be recalled. Many of the programmes were criticized for their triviality and the boredom they induced. Life adjustment provoked, in reaction, the subject-centred curriculum projects of the 1950s and 60s. These projects have not proved to be a satisfactory way of bringing about educational reform in a mass system. We are in a position to plan effectively for mass secondary and continuing education, provided we attend to the problem of finding appropriate ways of embodying educational criteria in our work at every stage.

In attempting to frame educational criteria by which curriculum changes may be judged, we need to replace 'want satisfaction' with a standard that is distinctively human and sufficiently comprehensive to include the diverse forms of human value and achievements. It must not be so narrowly defined as to lead us to the conclusion that there are large numbers of 'ineducabley' people in our midst. The reduction of a comprehensive criterion of human worth to rationality has been attempted by Peters. This reduction and some of the ambiguities to which it has led have been criticized, and the debate on this subject continues. A central issue in this debate is the nature of the interrelationships among rational and emotional qualities of experience.

Education is a process of qualitative transformations of experience which are structured by the principal enduring modes of cultural expression and achievement. Educational criteria are indigenous to these cultural modes and represent the progressive assimilation of, critical response to, and projection of these modes. The search for value, for experiences that have depth, resonance, continuity and the power to stimulate intense efforts of imaginative thought, has resulted in a great richness and diversity of forms of expression. These forms of expression include but go beyond the knowledge domains. The Western idea of rationality, formed under the profound influence of conceptual thought and scientific empiricism, is only one form of expression, although, in our experience, it is one of the most pervasive and persuasive. There are others, including the arts and styles of interpersonal relationships and social intercourse distinctive of particular cultural traditions. It is a violation and a distortion of the Western forms of cultural expression to reduce them to what is all too recognizable, educationally, in the framework of the grammar school curriculum. In this curriculum, which has exerted a deep and lasting influence on the curriculum in all kinds of schools, the discursive modes of language, science and history have achieved a dominance both over the content of the curriculum as a whole and its structure. For example, the school timetable is far more congenial to didactic types of classes and laboratory teaching than to workshop studies, field-based activities and social experience. Both curriculum and school power are exercised by the proponents of the discursive tradition, who naturally tend to judge all other contenders for space in the cultural arena from their own particular standpoint. One advantage to be gained from the apparently abstract task of defining educational critera with reference to the diverse forms of human experience, is that a much richer source of curriculum materials would become available than is now in common use.

Openness and structure: from whose standpoint?
Reference to the use made of pre-established standpoints in assessing the worth of new curriculum proposals is a reminder that curriculum may appear more or less open or structured according to one's point of view. From the teacher's standpoint a curriculum may appear open in the following ways:

1 It provides for free pupil choice within a defined range of activities.
2 Outcomes are ineffable, not fully predictable in advance, hence 'open-ended'.
3 It provides him with scope, e.g. it is open to him to change, it is an important part of his self-chosen professional life-space; it provides him with 'openings', i.e. professional contacts and associations; it liberates him intellectually and provides a constant stimulus to this thought.

However, from the pupil's standpoint, that same curriculum may have quite different meanings:

1 It mystifies him by substituting alien and incomprehensible constructs for his familiar perceptions.

2 It constraints and directs his action.

3 It is open to him only to make minor choices within what appears to him a pre-ordained structure.

4 Its structure is constantly obscured by its factual foreground.

These are extreme examples of both teacher and pupil perceptions. The citation of more typical situations may reveal a wider community of perception and task embracing teacher and pupil. There is also, in this illustration, a danger of equating openness with freedom, and structure with control. In the cultural world, freedom is achieved by grasping, using, and re-making structures, not by disengaging oneself and floating off into an imaginary space of unlimited choices. In the curriculum, openings present themselves in the pursuit of programmes. Left to himself, in a kind of limbo, the child discovers nothing, achieves no freedom. Yet the pupil's perceptions of the curriculum are no less important, pedagogically, than those of the teacher.

I have been suggesting that we attend to the ways in which pupil choices, their freedom of action, their growth in understanding, their autonomy as cultural agents, derive from and are inextricably related to the structures which characterize cultural modes. However, I have also pointed to the problems of defining situations entirely from the standpoint of those within, or partially within them. Thus a curriculum may be structured, according to the behaviouristic conventions, by operational objectives, units of learning, pre-arranged resource materials and assignment schedules. But this structure may be far less visible and far less meaningful to pupils than the teacher supposes it to be. After all, he (the teacher) has become familiar with its structures by making and re-making it. The students, as it were, are only passing through, and miss half the signposts. It is obvious that if it is the understanding of a structure, and of the process of structuring, that we are concerned with, then the pupils themselves need to be orientated towards structure and process. One of the dangers of the recent emphasis on 'the structure of knowledge' in curriculum development is that it is the curriculum designers who thereby educate themselves, leaving the rest – teachers as well as pupils – to pick up the crumbs. Professor Bruner, for instance, must be a lot better educated than those who teach and study 'Man : A Course of Study'.

In considering the questions, 'How do we structure the curriculum?' and 'How do we achieve openness in a structured curriculum?', we need to consider who is to be involved, and how, in the structuring processes. Cultural freedom, which arises from knowledge, experience and engagement, will continue to be very unevenly distributed if, in the management of schooling, we continue to leave the curriculum planning decisions in the hands of a tiny minority. But we can hardly do otherwise when our structures of decision-making are so primitive. No less primitive is the view, still widely entertained, that at some point, an individual qualifies to begin taking decisions. This is like the claim sometimes made in teaching morals and religion, that first comes the substance to be learned, and then comes the inquiry – just about to begin at the time pupils leave school. Curriculum planning need not be confined to a small team of specialists, but can involve all those concerned from the outset. This planning is itself a form of inquiry.

Structuring the curriculum for cultural freedom: some issues and possibilities

The difficulty of planning for freedom in the curriculum and the abortive efforts of many curriculum theorists to give sensible accounts of what they have been about has led some thinkers into a predictable scepticism. Immersion in the classroom and a view of the world from the standpoint of the classroom are sometimes recommended as alternatives to systematic thought. This recommendation is as dangerous as the dichotomy between theory and practice, since it ignores the fact that the classroom has no ultimate educational significance, and is only one standpoint among many of which theories have to take account. No less significant is the related fact that the classroom itself, like every concrete phenomenon, must be interpreted.

This is not of course to deny the importance of the classroom, within our present institutionalized arrangements, as both the locus of curriculum activities and the testing ground for ideas. Thus, structuring the curriculum implies designing the class as a learning unit, equipping the classroom and the school as a learning system, and preparing the teacher as a curriculum developer. The latter point is of crucial importance in the English system, which confers considerable freedom on the teacher.

Are there, then, models for application in these design and preparation situations? Do we possess strategies for changing our structures? The well known so-called rational planning model, derived from the industrial and military cultures but also, in an odd way, from the progressive education tradition, (via the work of Tyler), is often recommended as such a strategy. If there are, as I have suggested, distinctive modes of human experience which serve to articulate the major substantive decisions in curriculum-making, it would be strange for them not to impinge upon methodological questions. Rational curriculum planning, as already noted, seems to fit all, it fits them in different ways. Professor Hirst developed this point in his conference paper. If we are concerned about open culture, in the sense of cultural pluralism and diversity, then we should be looking very closely at the various possibilities that are open to us in structuring the curriculum. I shall conclude by identifying some of them, inserting one or two questions in the process. These possibilities are not mutually exclusive, nor are they equally open to us in all educational situations.

1 The curriculum is planned and its outcomes are assessed as a totality. This planning may be based on pre-specified behavioural objectives, which both derive from and reformulate clear intellectual structures of some description, e.g. physics.

2 How far precisely defined behavioural outcomes are appropriate, e.g. in the arts or in moral education, is debatable, but this is a separate issue from that of whole curriculum planning using a means-ends model. The curriculum is divided into major arenas, each of which is planned as in (1). These arenas may be the separate modes of experience, or they may be institutional devices, such as year groups.

3 The curriculum is so planned as to provide scope for a wide range of cultural action systems, each of which carries on its affairs and develops according to internal criteria. These criteria are not additive and they are, strictly speaking, incommensurable.

4 The curriculum is divided into a compulsory core and a set of electives. But what are the criteria by which we make this distinction, and how do we relate the core curriculum to the cultural needs of our time?

5 The range of curriculum offerings is broadened to promote pupil choice. How, then, and on what basis, do we establish a balanced curriculum?

6 The teacher is a major focus of curriculum development efforts. His lifelong education is treated as the best investment in curriculum change, and his ideas about structure and openness, thus developed, prevail in curriculum decision situations. Can all teachers reasonably be expected to act as curriculum developers? What are the roles of local, regional and national agencies?

7 Structures are seen to be emergent, the consequence of interactions between pupils, teachers and others. These interactions are subject to ongoing assessment through the application of educational criteria which are formulated with explicit reference to the different modes of experience.

8 Structures are produced which interrelate the elements of some of the principal cultural domains, as in ideological interpretations of

sets of phenomena (e.g. Marxism, Freudianism). These structures, while heavily interpretative, open up the possibility of fresh insights. This is achieved by invoking powerful explanatory concepts such as historical determinism and the unconscious, which have a re-orientating effect on the lives of those who assimilate them.

9 Individualized curriculum structures are a pedagogical requirement, but our mass systems of education have not achieved, indeed may even stand in the way of achieving, learning guides and procedures whereby children can make their way through the curriculum in their own style.

Conclusion

The possibilities I have identified in the preceding sections are not exhaustive, they are not systematically arranged, and I have not subjected them to critical scrutiny. Nevertheless, they are capable of detailed elaboration, and they could easily be illustrated from contemporary experience in many schools. In discussing them we would quickly penetrate some of the major issues in curriculum thinking: the value of the pre-designed course package; the nature of the distinctive knowledge domains and modes of experience; the advantages and disadvantages of pre-specified objectives; the role of the school in curriculum development; the factors that inhibit or enhance the success of particular curriculum changes; teacher planned integrations versus pupil responsibility for integrative thinking; the separation of 'key' elements in cultural structures from those which are merely 'incidental'; and the proper scope for teacher and pupil choice in curriculum matters. The interpenetration of theory and practice in the curriculum field will be revealed by the analysis of these and related issues.

Some Restraints Affecting Curriculum Development

JACK WALTON
University of Exeter

> Embedded in every school timetable is some view of what the curriculum is and what its objectives are. Sometimes the assumptions implicit in the timetable have been well pondered upon, sometimes not, but, whichever is the case, every curriculum reveals some basic assumptions, both by what it includes and by what it leaves out, how it arranges sequences and so on. In the comprehensive school timetable the issues at stake are even more complex than those of the timetable of either the grammar or the secondary modern school and the task of welding it together so as to fit complex requirements and make of it one coherent whole is even more difficult than for the other schools. (Halsall 1973)

I have chosen to open this paper with a quotation from the most recent book which has seriously considered the school curriculum. Elizabeth Halsall in *The Comprehensive School* exemplifies some of the educational problems posed by the organization of time in secondary schools. A traditional time reality is frequently described which appears to confine a more relevant time reality within certain unacceptable boundaries. It seems that one of the inferences that arises from Halsall's descriptions and comments is that in the 1970s in secondary education certain constraints which should be regarded as problematic are regarded as quite immutable. Before this and other points are discussed, however, the arguments need further development.

The changing attitudes to time in education can best be observed in the primary rather than in the secondary field. Primary education as we know it has been until quite recently more constrained by external pressures than secondary education. The reasons lie in the dominant elementary and proletarian (see Young 1971) basis of primary schooling and the consequent subordination of primary teachers to external control, particularly that of local authorities. Until quite recently it was considered appropriate that the greater majority of the population in England should follow in their early years quite an instrumental and preceptual process of learning. The curriculum was confined within narrow parameters and the quality of learning bore little relationship to the quantity of instruction. The reorganization proposed by the first Hadow Report, implemented particularly during the 1930s, ensured that appropriate spaces were made available for homogeneous groups of children to proceed a little of the way together, but at a later stage to differentiate into those who would pass the scholarship – later the 11 + examination – those who would not. Generally the resources were those that were appropriate to perceptual learning. Some of the population of the country could contract out of this system by entering their children for various forms of private education.

In recent years there have been, for a number of reasons, certain relaxations in external control. The concept of educational administration by the local education authorities has changed. Secondary reorganization has more often than not resulted in the abolition of the 11 + examination. The new generation of primary headteachers and teachers has taken advantage of the opportunities presented to reconsider the way time has been allocated in order that opportunities could be given to curricula which wished to be more open. Consequent upon the modification of a traditional time arrangement were other modifications relating to the use of space and the use of resources.

Malcolm Skilbeck in his paper suggested that it was a violation and distortion of the Western idea to reduce it to what is all too recognizable, educationally, in the framework of the grammar school curriculum. I think I would agree with him but, while also underlining the stereotype which may be presented to us by the grammar school curriculum, would suggest in addition that most state educational institutions, whether they be in the secondary or the primary field, have tended to celebrate aspects of the Western tradition in almost caricature form. A move from a closed and rigidly tight system to a more open system may just be a more sensible interpretation of the present day Western ethos.

Time has been suggested previously as the independent variable within the educational institution. It should be remembered, of course, that an attitude to time within an institution may be dependent upon outside controls, for example examinations. Nevertheless the way schools structure time should not be taken for granted. The way it is broken up and allocated tells us something about the nature and sources of what the school values. It could be claimed that within educational institutions time has been reified – a reification based upon Western middle class concepts. Such has been the reification that other orientations appear as irrational deviants.

While Indian attitudes to time may quite naturally be accepted at least as different, within Western society and particularly English society there exist sub-groups whose time concept may be different from that imposed by the establishment but which are not as acceptable as the Indian. For example, the child's concept of time may be completely different from that of the adult, working class time different from middle class time. If we consider time in school as middle class time, one of its characteristics is its future orientation. Many of the clients it serves may not have this orientation. They are concerned with the here and now. In fact, the future orientation may only be satisfactory to a minority.

It has been inferred that some schools, particularly in the primary sector, have now managed to break away from certain time restraints. Many schools, however, are still subject to a very particular timetable. It could be suggested that this school timetable with its division into lesson periods means that only certain types of learning can take place. The number of periods in the week may also mean that only certain subjects can be taught and that these 'must be learned (and taught) in more or less the same way, irrespective of any tendency towards continuity or episodicity they may contain' (Open University 1972). The implications of this fragmentation mean that the classroom teacher has often little control of the time-space variable within which the educational encounter takes place. It has already been mentioned that the traditional timetable tends to create a milieu more appropriate to sequential learning of the content type and places an emphasis on temporal or subjective time rather than inner or subjective time. The very fragmentation of the timetable seems to have led to group rather than individual attention and conversely to individual or solitary rather than group learning.

Goodlad's comment seems to be very appropriate. 'Educators create machinery to serve their educational ends. At the outset, the relationship between the end of view and the tool or form created to serve it may be clear. In time, however, the quality of the fit often deteriorates. The ends change without accompanying modifications of the means. Or, the means are refined over and over without respect to the character of the ends until modifications or perpetuations of the machinery become an end in itself. The ultimate sterility occurs when these same technicians start perpetuating the machinery in the name of the creator who would recoil at the sight of what he purportedly wrought' (Goodlad 1966). Perhaps a glance at secondary education will bear out the points that Goodlad is making in the above quotation.

In the 'middle' years of schooling, 11–16, there appears to be a significantly different approach to the use of time as compared with primary or further and higher education. It relates to the use of slack. This concept, as used by Shaw, refers to that time which is not programmed (Shaw 1972). In the junior school it could refer to significantly large areas of the week which are given over to various self-directed activities. These periods of time are open areas which give both the teachers and the pupils opportunities for responding to the immediate idea which is going well. In higher education slack is denoted by free periods, private study, library periods, more often than not an increasing amount of time which can be used by the student at his own discretion. It is relatively recently that the junior school has built slack into its week's programming. The secondary school, particularly during the first five years, programmes all the time for all the pupils. There is no slack. It may be worth suggesting some of the reasons for the lack of slack in the secondary programme. These could be listed as follows:

1 The dominance of the secondary curriculum by the needs of the non-terminal student, expressed in outward terms by the O Level and CSE examinations.

2 The introduction during this century of an increasing number of subjects into the secondary school curriculum.

3 Secondary education, in an attempt to give a general education and at the same time attempt to qualify people for work or for further study, has found it necessary to tightly programme all its students for all the time, particularly between the years 11 and 16.

The interest of the middle school movement, particularly where these schools cover ages 9 to 13, is that two years of children are removed from tight programming. At the other end, after the age of 16, the pressure is to some extent removed not because examinations have disappeared, but because it is no longer considered necessary to teach the student all the time. Changes, however, are taking place in secondary education. Many schools no longer feel that pupils in the first year in an 11–18 school need to start a curriculum which is immediately geared to external examination requirements. In certain schools slack is appearing in Forms 1 to 3 leaving Years 4 to 5 as the area most dominated by a traditional pattern of time arrangement.

As Dearden implies, the arrangement of time within school is an organizational rather than a curriculum concept (Dearden 1971). Nevertheless the way time is organized has a determining influence, not only upon the way learning is conducted within the school, but also upon the way the curriculum is conceived. The traditional pattern of time organization, as inferred earlier, tends to result in standard time units, standard group sizes, established time allocations to the various disciplines, fairly rigid and standardized teaching spaces – on the whole, rather preceptual teaching with a fairly limited need for other resources. It could be suggested that, as far as educational organization is concerned, its origin lies in the problems presented by mass formal state education. A lot of children have to be taught, as economically as possible, that knowledge which society considers to be desirable. Until quite recently additional monies available for the formal education system have more often than not been invested in the development of this traditional time concept. In the 1930s the new, reorganized junior elementary schools were given more traditional spaces which enabled them to further refine the groupings of children so that each grouping attempted to be fairly homogeneous. The second Hadow Report (1931), with all its suggestions for modifications in the style of teaching, was passed by virtually unattended. Again, in the post-war rebuilding after 1945, while the new buildings were often quite different in shape, the conventional classroom pattern still remained.

Accompanying this architectural consistency was also a consistency in the type of materials used by teachers in the classroom. In this respect it is interesting to consider the development of audio-visual aids. The expression itself indicates a kind of additive philosophy. If the blackboard, chalk, textbook and exercise book were the amplifiers or projections of the teacher in the early years of formal state education, the other aids tended to be only more sophisticated and perhaps complicated members of the same set of amplifiers. Particularly since World War II schools have been wired to facilitate the more common use of some of these amplifiers. Large sums of money have been spent, first on wireless sets and later on television. Projectors of various kinds appeared in all kinds of schools, whether primary or secondary. That their use has increased cannot be denied. Nevertheless on the whole they have tended to be rather characteristic additions to a basically traditional textbook situation that have required a technical expertise which teachers on the whole have shown no great enthusiasm to acquire. The fairly recent Sussex survey (Mackenzie 1970) has indicated that, while large sums of money have been invested in items of audio-visual hardware, it has often been left unused, year after year, stacked on the stock cupboard shelves.

The curriculum of both primary and secondary schools seems to contain ingredients originating in certain specific attitudes to knowledge and infers certain kinds of relationships between the teacher and the child. The over-riding organization of this kind of

I

curriculum in terms of specific time modules has so reified nodules in the minds of the teaching profession that, in Goodlad's sense, the machinery has become perpetuated from year to year as an end in itself. In the secondary school the timetable modifications that have been made have tended, until recently, to represent an attempt to extend the capabilities of the present machinery rather than to query the suitability of the machinery to meet the needs of students of the 1970s. Streaming, setting and options are common timetable terms expressive of this adaptive process. Primary schools, because they are smaller, have never needed to go to these extents. Recently they have acquired certain freedoms not possessed by the secondary school and have been able both to question the machinery and sometimes reject it completely.

The inference throughout this paper has been that time is the independent variable. If the time concept is radically changed, then many other variables in the teaching situation also change. An example could very well be the integrated day in the junior school. It is difficult to locate any really characteristic forms of the integrated day. Some schools have no timetables at all and relate the programmes of learning to the interests of the children as they appear to the teacher. Other schools set timetable for some of the time, leaving a good deal of time for more individual work. It is, however, only relatively recently that the English junior school has wished to move in this direction. Contributory factors have been released from the 11+ examination, a greater freedom from the control of the local authority, and, as a result of the release from these two constraints, an opportunity to follow up new educational ideas. The growing popularity of this movement towards a more open education has also been the result of the publicity given to experiments in particular schools, (for example, in Oxfordshire and Leicestershire), and to the work of a number of individuals. The term 'open education' is now becoming quite common. To quote Barth, 'Open education is a way of thinking about children, about learning and about knowledge: it is characterized by openness. There is a physical openness of schools. Doors are ajar, children come and go in the space within the school and without. Classrooms are open and children bring objects of interest to them in and take objects of interest out. Space in the open classroom is not preempted by desks and chairs organized in rows or in any other way. There is a variety of spaces filled with a variety of materials. Children move in this openness from place to place, from activity to activity. Both the world inside and outside the school is accessible to them. Space is fluid and changes with changing needs. The curriculum is open – open to choices by adults and by children as a function of the interests of children. The curriculum is the dependent variable – dependent upon the child rather than the independent variable upon which the child must depend' (Barth 1968). The American who wrote this was, of course, specifically referring to certain English primary schools. It is interesting to note that he describes the curriculum in the open school as a dependent variable. The thesis of this paper has been that time has been the independent variable upon which both the child and the curriculum have depended. The movement in recent years, particularly in primary schools, has been to modify the attitude to time, thus enabling the curriculum to relate more to the needs and interests of the children. However, a move to this openness can be accompanied by all kinds of difficulties, often resulting in disenchantment on the part of those involved. The problem that arises from any major modification of the independent variable, time, is that all other associated dependent variables are themselves modified. Bernstein describes the shifts in emphasis and change in teacher and pupil roles in the open situation (Bernstein 1971). He looks at it in terms of a change in the arrangement of knowledge rather than a change in the arrangement of time. Some possible results which he visualizes theoretically are as follows :

1 a shift in the pattern of work relationships – vertical to horizontal and some weakening of existing hierarchical vertical structures;
2 a weakening of the boundary between staff and students;
3 a change in the property concept of knowledge;
4 a change in the attitude towards the structure of knowledge;
5 the creation of homogeneity in teaching practice;
6 a reduction of the discretion of the individual teacher paralleled by the increased discretion of the pupils;
7 a movement from the didactic theory of learning to a group of more subregulated theory of learning;
8 a change in the structure of teaching groups which is likely to exhibit considerable flexibility;
9 a need in the move towards a greater openness for a highlevel of ideological consensus among the staff involved;
10 a greater ability to tolerate and enjoy the end ambiguity of the level of knowledge of social relationships;
11 the development of multiple criteria in assessment compared with the kind of assessment associated with the more traditional forms of teaching.

The traditional attitude to time in schools has been largely pragmatic in the sense that it has been arranged in such a way as to include in the curriculum that which society has considered essential. The knowledge has also been phased and the children grouped in order that that knowledge can be speedily and efficiently acquired. The modifications in grouping – for example, by setting and streaming – have been introduced to make this process more efficient. The changes proposed in the 1960s and 70s, however, are far more revolutionary in nature and do not necessarily accept the premises behind the more traditional structure of education. Unstreaming, subject integration and the integrated day all represent a movement towards openness which is fundamentally in conflict with the long-established modes of behaviour in formal state education. Traditional timetables can accommodate pragmatic maneuvres but are unable to cope with ideological pressures. It is because adequate modifications on traditional lines are becoming more and more impossible that the new structures, as indicated in the integrated day primary school, represent a complete departure from the past rather than a continuation of the past. For this reason there are many attendant consequences both in terms of material and human resources.

It has been suggested earlier that the constraints of a traditional time schedule impose upon both teacher and learner certain sequences of behaviour that put the teacher into the position of dispensing knowledge in a certain kind of way. If the strictures of time are removed and the teachers given greater flexibility to maneuvre, not only can the teaching be changed but more often than not new types of resources are required and new types of space arrangements suggested. Referring again to the junior school, consequent upon experiments with various forms of the integrated day, there have appeared new architectural forms generally classified as open plan schools. Secondary education, as a result of its immediacy to employment or full-time education, has been more restrained. As a result, only partial experiments have been attempted within the constraints of the existing timetable. However, by reconsidering the basis of timetable construction it is now possible to provide time spans which are considerably larger than formerly, and which are tending to approximate, if only in a partial sense, to those time spans of some primary schools. It would seem that in the next few years far more revolutionary inroads into secondary timetabling will be made.

Assuming the considerable modifications of the independent variable of time it seems reasonable to suggest that the two other curriculum restraints, the availability of appropriate resources and the buildings within which the learning encounters take place, will themselves have to alter. Perhaps these two restraints could be taken separately.

Earlier it was mentioned or inferred that with the traditional timetable, resources are additive. A move into a more open situation suggests that resources become far more an integral part of curriculum planning. The appearance in recent years of the National Council for Educational Technology, with its aim of making resource provision an integral part of curriculum development, suggests a national awareness of the more open curriculum movement which is taking place. If conventional resources within the traditional classroom have been quite meagre, they may nevertheless have been considered sufficient for the style of teaching which has been characteristically associated with, for example, the grammar school. If the move continues towards greater openness, the absence of appropriate resources could be catastrophic. The new resources should, in the Brunerian sense, be far more positive amplifiers of human experience. However, an important point is raised by Malcolm Skilbeck when he suggests that Bruner probably himself learnt more by his involvement in the 'Man : A Course of Study' programme than did the children. If resources are going to be more important in educational encounters, if development of a curriculum design associated with resources is itself a good learning experience, further questions are raised not only about the teacher's involvement in curriculum planning and development but also the pupil's involvement.

English school architecture has only relatively recently begun to change. Not surprisingly the first changes were in the primary field. 'Educational techniques involving integrated learning, project work, visual aids, intensive use of equipment, curricular studies, pastoral care and public participation, enabled the architect to develop planning as a functional distribution of space based on project analysis.... Nevertheless secondary school design based on rigid curriculum remained more formal....' (Spivey 1970) The traditional attitude to time distribution is associated with a certain kind of architecture. Change the attitude to time distribution and new kinds of more flexible spaces are required. The open plan school is the architectural response to the education decision to move towards an integrated day.

It has also been implied that the role of the teacher will change as a result of the modification of the time concept and the move towards more open education. If such a change is either envisaged or is taking place, it should be assumed that it is going to be accompanied by anxieties. There seems to be very little correspondence between styles of teaching in open education and those of more traditional education. Present day teachers have themselves been taught as pupils and more often than not have worked as teachers within a traditional structure. Old models of behaviour are difficult to cast aside. The movement towards open education and possible subsequent open plan buildings can often cause such anxiety that the teachers themselves arrange ad hoc modification of the open plan in order to restore the space arrangement to one similar to the more traditional pattern. In addition, if the teacher is going to be really effective in the open plan situation, he must not only take an effective part in curriculum planning but he must also be prepared to subordinate some of his views to those of his colleagues who are working with him. Some teachers faced with an architecturally open plan school will not accept this – they prefer to teach more in isolation and tend to modify the new building so that as far as possible it is comparable to the old. Spaces are filled in, other rearrangements are made and a simulated traditional classroom appears.

Malcolm Skilbeck, at the beginning of his paper, emphasizes structure. 'Rather than admitting a dichotomy between "structure" and "openness" which is educationally significant, I will argue that structures may be more or less open, and that educational situations, including curriculum situations, are never completely open.' I have been concerned with certain restraints, emphasizing the attitude to time as possibly that which is the most powerful. In attempting to outline the effects of what could be described as a 'container' revolution I have particularly emphasized a tendency to move to a greater openness from a traditional closed classroom pattern of teaching and learning. Unless teachers perceive the implications of the kinds of changes that have been described, unless they structure the openness according to criteria which they have developed, they may well not be involving themselves and their students in any valid kind of educational encounter. More open education requires of teachers a greater professionalism and a greater insight into the learning process. They must therefore take care when they meddle with the time machine.

References

BARTH, R. S. (1968) *Open Education: Assumptions and Rationale* Cambridge, Mass: Harvard Graduate School of Education
DEARDEN, R. (1971) What is the integrated day? *The Integrated Day*

in Theory and Practice London: Ward Lock Educational

GOODLAD, J. L. (1966) *School Curriculum and the Individual* Blaisdell

HALSALL, E. (1973) *The Comprehensive School* Oxford: Pergamon

MACKENZIE, N. (1970) Audio-visual resources in Sussex Schools *British Journal of Educational Technology* 1, 1

OPEN UNIVERSITY (1972) Course E282, *The Curriculum: Context Design and Development* Unit 7, *The Use of Time in the School prepared* by I. R. Dale.

SHAW, K. E. (1971) Management and Innovation in Education *Curriculum Organization and Design* London: Ward Lock Educational

SPIVEY, C. A. (1970) 1870–1970: From teaching rooms to comprehensives *Education*, 27 November

YOUNG, M. F. D. (ed) (1971) *Knowledge and Control* London: Collier Macmillan

Section 5: Managing Innovation and Change

Introduction

JOHN HANSON
Oxford Education Authority

This section examined the many issues involved in the process of curriculum change and innovation. It recognized the need for organized strategies in school or college to manage the processes of innovation and change which necessarily generate interaction, even conflict, and are attended by stress. These strategies, it was argued, should be devised to stimulate consultation and cooperation and to harness creative energy and capability in a productive fashion.

Apathy was considered to be the main enemy. There was, it was thought, much to be learned about ways of arousing positive and intelligently critical attitudes towards innovation and change. In this respect the trend towards greater participation in management, with substantial sharing of power and responsibility, was to be welcomed as likely to be of benefit in creating situations which demanded involvement and commitment and which stimulated initiative throughout a school or college.

The role of the head or principal was seen to be crucial in creating conditions for innovation. Intelligent, perceptive and sensitive leadership was called for, as distinct from autocratic direction or the sort of leadership which relies on the charisma of a powerful personality. Agreement on the need for training and for outside support to assist schools in adapting their organization was general. Management training was considered to be equally necessary for LEA staff and others advising schools.

Noting that much curriculum development undertaken outside schools was not necessarily seen by teachers as relevant or of value, it was generally agreed that someone professionally acceptable from outside the school organization, a 'change agent' could provide a stimulus and support to schools in promoting curriculum development. There is plenty of evidence of the successes which can be achieved by use of a 'change agent' who appreciates how schools or colleges work and what their needs are.

Attention was drawn to other factors which can either foster or inhibit change: the school timetable can be a straitjacket but it need not be; blocking in large units can provide opportunities for cooperative curriculum planning and development and thereby widen the educational opportunities for the pupils. Ill-designed resources for learning or resources which are not used efficiently and effectively can be counter-productive and may militate against change and innovation. Flexibility in building design is supportive of change, though many old buildings are perfectly adaptable to change. Faculties or departments, too, can be organized in ways which are not necessarily divisive.

Frequent mention was made in discussion of the stress experienced by teachers who are involved in curriculum development (the more so where change is, or seems to be, imposed) and of the very heavy demands made on teachers' time. There is some evidence that it is difficult for a teacher to sustain innovation for more than about three years. The need for teacher replacement and time for planning to be built into the school programme seems essential if innovation and development are to be sustained effectively.

Machinery for managing change, particularly in large schools, needs to avoid over-elaborate communication procedures which can take up much time and energy and divert the drive that should be devoted to creative development. But machinery is necessary, or so the section considered, if innovation and change is to become a functional part of educational institutions.

The two papers presented to the section, one a general exposition of a systems approach to issues of innovation and change and the other a case study, both emphasize the need for a critical awareness of the organizational processes in which teachers and headteachers, administrators and policy-makers engage.

Educational Need and Organization

GORDON E. WHEELER
Combe Lodge Further Education Staff College

Some organizations change haphazardly by what is described as organizational drift. That is, organizations evolve, adjust and readjust seemingly unaffected by the conscious efforts of their members. The antithesis of the drift phenomena is planned change. Here, organizational change takes place as a result of conscious rational efforts by those individuals who control the organizations. Understanding both kinds of organizational change, their characteristics and their interrelationships, should enable a person to combat the harmful side effects of organizational structures and processes. When we think of an educational system supposedly designed to fulfil educational ends or needs, we must recognize that any organizational system is likely to have side effects which themselves may completely destroy the opportunity of fulfilling educational needs, just as a drug meant to be curative may, to those who are sensitive, be a poison.

I am thinking of the educationist – the teacher, the head of department, the tutor, the Chief Education Officer – as significantly a person who fulfils an educational need by creating a way, an organization, a system, by which this end is both identified and satisfied. We cannot, certainly as teachers, consider an educational need to be satisfied without an educational system, since without a system no teachers, as a professional group that is, would exist. One international observer has attempted to establish a model which may help us to think through the problem of modifying systems, organizations, schools, call them what you will, in such a way that they meet identified needs (Griffiths 1957). We must remember that even stability is, paradoxically enough, a position of change. For an organization to maintain its position in a changing environment, with a changing set of students, with changing economic and social pressures, different stances must be adopted.

Indeed, the tendency of organizations is to maintain a steady state. The major impetus for change comes from outside rather than inside an organization. Griffiths's propositions are as follows:

1 That the major impetus for change in an organization is from the outside, and one may argue that when change in an organization does occur, the initiative for the change is from outside the system, that is, from what may be called the supra-system. Practical educationists are well aware of this proposition. The use of consultants, evaluation teams, advisory committees or professional organizations to bring change to an institution suggest a clear recognition on the part of education administrators that an organization is more apt to change in response to an external force than to an internal one.

2 The degree and duration of change is directly proportional to the intensity of the stimulus from the supra-system. One only has to think of the effect upon technological education by the launching of Sputnik.

3 Change in an organization is more probable if the successor to the Head or Principal is from outside the organization than if he is from inside. The reason for this is not difficult to discover. The man who comes in from outside does not receive feed-back from his actions, since well established channels for feed-back to him do not exist. When an insider is appointed to the top post of an organization, the feed-back channels which have been established over the years function to keep him operating in the steady state. The insider will also keep the sub-systems functioning without conflict since he knows how these sub-systems function to maintain the steady state. An outsider may bring change into an organization out of sheer ignorance. Not knowing the system, he will function in terms of the system which he does know. Being without ties in the system, he will not receive a feed-back that would keep him from initiating procedures and policies differing from those in use. Not knowing the sub-systems, he can inadvertently throw them into conflict through orders or expectations not customarily held for these systems. On the other hand he may introduce conflict among the sub-systems by purposefully changing their function. This will, of course, upset the steady state and may in time create a state more to the liking of the Head. The notion of controlled conflict as a method of change in an organization may have a sound theoretical base. One must realize therefore, that the likelihood of a change of structure is greater under an outsider, and must question whether the establishment of an academic board, which consists primarily of insiders, will bring about the changes which have been frequently hypothesized both by those within and outside the organization. In fact, there is some evidence that there is often a strenuous effort by those inside an organization to create situations in which the existing state can be encompassed within the actions of an academic board.

4 Living systems respond to ever-increasing stress, first by a

lagging response, then by an over-compensatory response and finally by catastrophic collapse. If we look at this in terms of current educational situations, we can argue that institutions are not at first aware of new educational needs, but once these have been identified, the system tries to turn very rapidly to satisfy these needs, e.g. provision of education for scientists. We may hypothesize catastrophic collapse if we continue to use our resources to train potential scientists and technologists at the current rate, we shall have an increasing expenditure on resources which have no feed-back. Of course, the scientists may be used for other purposes. In another area one may reflect on the great efforts to sell Concordes to China which has apparently resulted in an agreement to exchange Chinese dried rabbits for British technology. One wonders whether an initial investment of the technology in producing dried rabbit or, preferably fresh beef, would not have been more of a satisfaction to the participants in the system! Many of the characteristics of organizations are such that they make the initiation of change difficult. When organizations are viewed in terms of the system they model, these characteristics show up very clearly.

5 'The number of innovations is inversely proportional to the tenure of the Chief Administrator.' The reason for this has something, at least, to do with the frequency of interaction between sub-systems. Where this inter-action is decreased because each sub-system has found its position, the chances of effective communication are diminished. Without effective communication, the chance for change also diminishes.

6 Griffiths argues that the more hierarchial the structure of an organization, the less the possibility of change. Here we might examine in our own terms the new 'traditional' hierarchical system we are attempting to establish in educational institutions. In the past there existed the hierarchy of normal school or college structure, but to this we now add the hierarchy of committees. Individuals, sub-committees, working groups reporting to main committees, reporting to academic boards, reporting to Governors – each committee rests firmly within a structure system. As each part of the hierarchy gains independence of the others because of the hierarchy composition, the more complex and more difficult the job of introducing change to the system. When one hears an educationist say, 'this matter must be referred to a committee,' at least one can be certain that there will be no rapid changes!

7 'When changes in the organization do occur, they will tend to occur from the top down, not from the bottom up.' Structures tend to make changes from the bottom up difficult. Foundations may collapse but the super-structure is self supporting. This, incidentally,

may be a reason why those of us who have had ambitions to see things differently also must necessarily have ambitions to be a top man, to see the different things actually brought about. One only has to look at a communication system to see that these are always designed to ensure rapid communication from the top down and not from the bottom up. The man at the top can sort out the priorities of the man at the bottom in a way which the man at the bottom can seldom do for the man at the top.

The last of Griffiths's propositions is more functional: 'The dynamic interplay of sub-systems lessens change in organization.' This is because each of the sub-systems has a function to perform and each does so in a manner which will allow it to maintain a high degree of harmony with others. Each sub-system says to the others in effect, 'if you don't rock the boat I won't.' Change is practically synonymous with conflict since it means that the arrangements for sub-systems as worked out no longer hold true. Sub-systems resist conflict and in the same manner resist change. Of course one of the arts of change-management in this situation is to threaten to rock the boat if the other chap doesn't move his position a little to enable something which you want to take place to occur. The risk is that the other chap could rock your boat while you are bringing the change about, and he only waits for a practical opportunity to do so.

Now what is this all to do with educational need and educational systems? It is that in recognition of the need, we have to take account of the systems which we must necessarily live with. Of course this may lead to fairly anarchistic feelings, at least in questioning some of the propositions upon which organizations are built up. In one recent study on organizational stress, we are reminded that in fact the concepts we have about good organizations 'all ship-shape and Bristol fashion', are very often concepts which seem most likely to maximize stress situations (Berger *et al* 1964). One might even think of the process of 'annealing' organizations or annealing processes for organizations. What are these stresses? One of the most common stresses in the organization is its interplay with other organizations at its boundaries; indeed, with the outside world. An organization is recognized in theoretical terms by its boundary, and you can clearly see a school or college in these terms.

There are five recommendations which may be made about the management of organizational stress, although one must remember that the elimination of a single source of stress often brings side effects in the form of new and still stressful imbalances. For example, the appearance of academic boards in colleges has not necessarily reduced the stress situation of Principals and Heads of Department who have executive responsibilities. It has certainly enlarged the opportunities for stressful relationships between Principals and the Governing Body, between the local authority and college officers and between the college, its Governors and its committees. Such relationships were simpler, at least, before Circular 7/70 (DES 1970). However, let us look at what we can do to reduce difficulties in trying to meet educational needs through organizational development.

Firstly, the problem of stress seems always to arise at the boundary of organizations between college and school, between one department and another, even between one course and another. All of these are boundary situations, and here it would seem that it is necessary to create specialized positions within organizations. These positions must be strongly supported in terms of power, ancillary services and organizational recognition. The chap who goes along to a committee must have been delegated some powers of decision-making at least. Multiple liaison relationships are less stressful than single ones, all truth is seldom contained in one approach and there must be a way for those who dwell, as it were, at the boundary to be integrated with those who are active inside the organization. In other words, if a department has one person who is liaison officer with another department, it does not mean that the liaison has occurred between all the people in both departments. In the same way the designated course tutor who has liaison responsibilities between a college and a group of students may not succeed in establishing liaison for the institution. This, of course, may be one of the disadvantages in having a system in which counselling and guidance are singled out as unique functions – indeed the tutor may be organizationally 'seduced' and 'join' the group he is responsible for.

A second proposal for minimizing stress is in the structural design of organization. This has to do with size, shape and requirements of co-ordination or (a more popular word in our language now) comprehensiveness or 'comprehensibilization'. It would seem that as organizations grow, and certainly to be comprehensive they must grow, stressfulness increases. There is a good deal of research evidence to indicate this. Graicunas first drew attention to this, and most of us have become aware of the kind of arithmetical problems of co-ordination which can arise with growth. Thus for two persons there is only one bond, for three persons three bonds, four persons six bonds, five, ten bonds, and so on, and this is an acceleration of strain. The implication of all this, for those of us who are responsible organizers, is to minimize the requirement for co-ordination between people, between positions and groups. In other words, instead of regarding co-ordination as an advantage again, treat it as a cost, which it is. We should make every unit as autonomous as it can be and where a co-ordinative bond has to exist, we should seek to establish the minimum number of activities which must be co-ordinated in order to avoid undue organizational risks.

Of course, if I advocate minimum co-ordination, this contrasts strongly with the notion of centralized leadership, and here again, using an example from our colleges, the role of the academic board in acting in a co-ordinative way is in this direction suspect. It is interesting to reflect that the essential nature of the teacher as an individual professional has at least some theoretical support organizationally in this concept of co-ordinative cost. The professional who can act on his own initiative and in his own way in the light of the pragmatic problems which he faces, without reference to anyone else, obviously has the minimum of co-ordinative requirements for himself and his position. This of course does not prevent him from creating stresses for others. A collection of professionals each acting upon one individual is something which is quite often quite terrifying. Of course the suggestion that co-ordination is a cost is not likely to be very popular with those of us who hold managerial status, since most of us who are managers spend most of our time co-ordinating, or at least attempting to. If co-ordination has to be reduced, then presumably managers have either got to find something more useful to do (and there are plenty of things here), or they will find themselves with nothing to do, which tends to give managers an enormous guilt complex! If we want co-ordination then it has got to be built in to the system rather than being forced upon it, and we must pay special attention to two things: the setting of objectives and the reward structure. Deutsch distinguishes between two kinds of interdependence which he calls *promotive* and *contrarient* (Deutsh and Krauss 1965). Persons or groups are promotively inter-dependent when the success of one facilitates the success of the other. Members of a football team, for example, are promotively inter-dependent. The joys and rewards of victory can come only through collaborate effort, (though some of them seem to forget this), and they exist for all members of the team.

The idea of reward would follow the same line in that we should ensure that rewards are given for fulfilling organizational objectives. Here, in a side comment, one might think of the present situation in the Polytechnics where it appears that the highest rewards are given not to teaching activity but for academic distinction. I remember being told that the Polytechnics would be different from the universities in having a high emphasis upon teaching capacity. We learned, only recently, of the problems associated with teaching the mentally handicapped, where the chances of any educative processes are very low. I have to wonder what the chances would be if the rewards for teaching the mentally disabled were in any way equal to the rewards of teaching the mentally able. Researchers elsewhere, of course, have noticed that the greatest stresses and frustrations in industrial settings derive from reward systems which were at variance either with concepts of equity, as between one person and another, or with the stated or apparent objectives of the organization.

A third area of stress is that in the field of communications. Practically every educationalist will argue about the difficulties of the communicative processes and most of us in organizations tend to feel that we are not communicated to enough about the right things. I would suggest that this is symptomatic not of communications but the way in which they are organized. Primarily, I think it is not that we want to be told, *we want to ask*. Yet most of us spend a great deal of time being told when we want to tell. Think of the poor student in the classroom – unless he is extremely lucky he has to endure being told for a thousand or more hours a year, while we as teachers indulge in the managerial luxury of telling him. Of course, we know best what he should be told, just as everyone who tells *us* knows best what we should be told, but I notice within us acute critical capacity in terms of the DES, the local authorities, Lord Longford or whoever happens to be telling us at any particular moment. Communication systems in general are organized so that people can be told. Very rarely can those who are told most respond by telling. There are lessons in this to be found in the educational process, which is essentially one of learning and not of being taught. It is the learner who needs to do the asking and, indeed, the telling, rather than the teacher.

The processes of educational administration must always be supportive of the educational needs they are meant to satisfy. This paper has tried to show how frequently organizational factors influence both the provision and effectiveness of the educational service.

References

BERGER, R *et al* (1964) *Organizational Stress* New York : John Wiley

DEPARTMENT OF EDUCATION AND SCIENCE (1970) *Government and Conduct of Establishments of Further Education* Circular 7/70 London: HMSO

DEUTSCH, M. and KRAUSS, R. M. (1965) *Theories in Social Psychology* New York: Basic Books

GRIFFITHS, D. E. (1957) Toward a Theory of Administrative Behaviour in *Administrative Behaviour in Education* Campbell and Gregg (eds) New York: Harper & Row

Additional reading

BARON, G. and TAYLOR, W. (Eds) (1969) *Educational Administration and the Social Sciences* London: Athlone Press

CAMPBELL, R. F. and GREGG, R. T. (Eds) (1957) *Administrative Behaviour in Education* New York: Harper & Row

GETZELS, J. W., LIPHAM, J. M. and CAMPBELL, R. F. (Eds) (1968) *Educational Administration as a Social Process* New York: Harper & Row

KAHN, R. L., WOLFE, D. M., QUINN, R. P., SNOEK, J. D., and ROSENTHAL, R. A. (Eds) (1964) *Organizational Stress* New York: John Wiley

K

Countesthorpe: A Case Study

JOHN WATTS
Principal, Countesthorpe College, Leicestershire

To be of use to anybody other than those directly involved, a case study of Countesthorpe would need to throw some light on such questions as these:

1 What are the prerequisites for embarking on a large-scale innovation?
2 Among these prerequisites, how important in particular are changes in personal relationships within the school?
3 What are the principal initial constraints, and which are most likely to be overlooked?
4 What are the most likely resultant obstacles? Which of these need to be surmounted rapidly? Which are likely to be long-term problems?
5 From what directions can initiative for innovation be expected?
6 Can an innovating school maintain momentum? What are the conservative forces most likely to emerge?
7 Under what circumstances, if any, could Countesthorpe serve as a possible model?

Bearing these questions in mind, I want to outline first what the stated intentions were at the outset, then what distinctive innovations have occurred, what problems these have given rise to, what solutions have been arrived at, and, finally, what serious obstacles still remain. In this way, some attempt can be made to answer the questions and to provide illustration of some at least of the principles set out in Wheeler's paper.

Tim McMullen, first Warden (Principal) of Countesthorpe, was able to pick the initial staff in time to work out with them the practical application of their common aims. In an early paper he was able to say this: 'Unlike the normal situation, we have a chance to rethink the total process of learning within the school, subject only to the demands made by outside institutions – i.e. universities, parents – and the personal material resources available to us. This does not mean that everything we do will be different from what has been done before, but it should mean that we do not automatically repeat an established practice without considering why.'

He then went on to state certain major objectives that could be proposed in relation to the 16-year-old. Each of these carries extensive implications for the individual teacher and for the school as an institution, but what is important here is a realization that our starting point at Countesthorpe was, quite properly, an overriding concern for the needs of the student.

McMullen emphasized that a precondition for the achievement of any curriculum objectives was the creation by staff of optimum conditions for effective motivation on the part of students. This was important as it established a different emphasis from that of anyone who might claim that learning should stand at the top of our priorities in curriculum objectives without recognizing that a whole realm of social relationships need to be established in school before that learning can occur. The kinds of motivation to be sought were twofold : internal, to be derived from intrinsic satisfactions in work done well according to the student's own lights; and external, first in advancing some long-term aim in examinations and career, second in pleasing others upon whom there is social dependence – parents, teachers and peer-group. It goes without saying, though I have myself found that it needs saying over and over again to anyone outside the circles of those truly committed to comprehensive education, that these needs for effective motivation extend to the whole range of school students and not just to a few nice kids who have supposedly 'got it up there'. I mention this because there is a tendency to underestimate the strength of the overriding desire of most adolescents to please the peer-group.

Five main areas of curriculum objectives were then outlined : Knowledge, Logical Processes, Skills, Creative and Expressive Actions, Personality Factors and Attitudes.

In considering knowledge, account was taken of the knowledge explosion and the principle of indeterminate relevance – that is, the extent to which we cannot foresee what knowledge, out of a constantly expanding total, will be significant at any future date. Consequently, the knowledge and understanding of facts, principles and concepts was envisaged as mainly relating to 'the student's knowledge of himself, of his relationships with others, both individuals and groups, of groups and their behaviour, of local, national and international aspects of society – in that order of importance,' and secondly to 'the student's knowledge of his environment and man's interaction with it.'

Under Logical Processes were grouped the intellectual skills of analysis, selection and synthesis, formation of hypothesis, testing for validity. One immediate implication was drawn: if the development of these processes was to occur, then we should depart from the usual limited practice of recall for relevance and construct a curriculum that introduced a heavy demand for problem-solving.

Skills, to be acquired by practice and modified by criticism, included Communication Skills, Executant Skills, Craft Skills and Physical Skills.

Creative and Expressive Actions, as a class, covered the original generative aspects of the arts, including plastic arts, words, music, drama, sport, and all the activities which involve lateral rather than convergent thinking.

The fifth class was essentially that of the Affective Domain, but named here as 'Personal Factors and Attitudes'. It detailed a number of objectives relating to understanding of the self and others, development of moral conduct, tolerance of the autonomy and morality of others, self-control, cooperation, valuing of distant goals and the organization of one's own work and play.

Most models put up for innovation start with a statement of objectives, though I suspect that in an ongoing situation it is more likely that innovation will start more or less spontaneously and give rise to a reappraisal of aims. It is only at times such as the opening of a new school that there is likelihood of conformity to the model of initial statements such as we were able to make. By and large these objectives have stood unchallenged and remain as the yardstick against which we measure our practice to assess any success. Curriculum needs to be measured against both effectiveness and validity so that eventually we shall need to scrutinize these objectives, and their balance of emphasis, in order to test their validity. After less than three years, however, it is sufficient perhaps to look at how effectively they have been put into practice.

The second stage of planning was to devise the working structures for such a curriculum. (For convenience I shall concentrate on the Upper School, in the 14 – 18 age range. Countesthorpe was complicated by having initially to cope with a High School element, 11–14 age range, and an Upper School that had to build up from 14-year-olds. Only after three years, in 1973/74 will it consist of the intended 14–18 year olds.) The original intention was to require all students to follow a balanced curriculum by including in it six departments. These were: 1 Study of the Individual and the Group (IG); 2 Creative and Expressive Work in Words, Music and Movement (CW); 3 Mathematics; 4 Science; 5 Creative and Expressive Work in two and three dimensional media (2D/3D); and 6 some form of physical activity. This was to form a core around which time could be added, depending on individual need, in Languages,

European Studies, and other subjects.

The staff framework for implementing and coordinating this was essentially a dual hierarchy under two Directors of Studies, one responsible for mathematics and sciences, the other for the humanities, creative and expressive work (including physical education). There were Assistant Directors of Studies, corresponding very much to heads of departments, in Maths, Biology, Physical Sciences, in the one branch ,and in the other for IG, CW, 2D/3D, and Languages. It was an unstable structure, calling unrealistically for polymatic capabilities in such yokings as Music and Movement under one Assistant Director of Studies for C.W. However, this was the original organization of studies, and it was predictable that early adjustments would follow from the interactions of the different personal characteristics of the people appointed to the various posts.

Even recognizing the instability of this coordinating structure, its major components, with their internal curriculum grouping, (such as IG with its elements of Sociology and History), had every chance of functioning. The architecture of the school allowed for a spatial relationship between departments that corresponded quite surprisingly to their theoretical interaction. (Thus it has been possible to develop Control Technology as a subject in a space that links the Physics labs of the Science area with the vehicle maintenance and heavy machine shop end of the craft workshops.) Moreover, the design gave us a variety of large open areas, allowing for subdivision with furniture. This was a necessary prerequisite for the style of work to be introduced.

In planning a new school, if there is any departure from established practice at all, it is most likely to appear in the organizational structure : how departments are grouped, what sort of academic cabinet or board of studies holds the intermediate level of power. This often results in new buildings with old blocks. In such a case it is rare that any reshaping will occur in the component blocks themselves; and less likely that anyone will ask 'How, if at all, will History and Geography feature in the curriculum, so as to achieve our stated objectives?' Rather, the problem will be 'What scale allowance will Head of History have, and where will he stand in the hierarchy?' It is of course, comparatively safe to limit innovation to this sort of shuffling, because for the pupil in the classroom, for subject-inspectors, for parents and local administration, the result is the same as before, with the same old things being taught in classrooms in the same old way, give or take a few audio-visual aids.

At Countesthorpe, though, the crucial feature was seen to be the relationship of student to teacher and the consequent kinds of learning that could take place. The whole emphasis was to switch from teacher-centred instruction to student-centred enquiry with the aim of maximizing the students' eventual autonomy. If the prerequisite to learning was to be effective motivation, then with a comprehensive intake the teachers would need to search diligently for what would interest or catch the imagination of the individual student, to expect diversity, and having found it, to cater for it. The implications of this were mainly twofold: the teacher needed to know his students individually and intimately, and he needed much more flexible resource backing than normal.

Recognizing the danger that individualizing study could lead to a greater intensity of spoon-feeding, this had to be done with the superordinate objective of autonomy kept in mind. Nevertheless, a radically different attitude on the part of teachers to students was seen to be essential. Normally teachers rely on social distance to exercise control of behaviour and study. It is a form of discipline appropriate to an expectation that pupils will conform to a teacher model, both in the selection of knowledge to be acquired and in the decorum of speech, dress and manners. We recognized that this is only likely to succeed where there is congruence of expectation as between parent and teacher, in a public school or grammar school, and that a major cause of alienation and hostility in a comprehensive school arises from teachers conflating their academic and social demands, while their pupils, particularly working-class pupils, sense rejection, inferiority and failure. To make autonomy even possible it was felt necessary to limit drastically the traditional school demands on its pupils for social conformity in terms of, say, uniform and submissive indicators in speech and manner. It was felt that a teacher could only deserve to acquire respect, not be accorded it. Above all, the teacher was to be accessible and ready to negotiate.

He had to be accessible and ready to negotiate so that the student could genuinely learn to exercise responsible choice. In learning this, the student needed guidance, and to give guidance the teacher had to know the individual's blockages, potentials, enthusiasms and fears. Such a relationship, growing only in trust and freedom from the exploitation of competitive methods, was incompatible with such common school features as queueing outside the staffroom, standing up straight and saying 'Please Sir' before being given permission to speak, or condemnation by teachers of styles of speech and dress accepted as normal at home. Furthermore, this relationship, although having its root justification in curriculum and style of learning, was seen to affect the very basis of government within school.

If we propose that students of fourteen and over should not only learn the meaning of autonomy but actually *become* autonomous, then we must accept that this cannot be confined for long to the selection of study areas within the curriculum. There are two clear reasons for this: first, our objectives were not confined to academic knowledge and cognitive skills, but rather laid great store by the acquisition of affective social skills and attitudes; second, the curriculum was not considered as just that which could be divided into subject syllabuses but was seen as the totality of intended learning situations. The corollary to this is that as much will be learnt from working within the school as a community as from the curriculum programmes. Indeed, unless a school is consistent in all its practices, between departments and outside them, in pursuing its objectives, the pupil is bound to be first confused and then alienated. Thus if a teacher says in class, 'In order that you should learn to think for yourselves, I am providing a problem to which you, between you, must find a solution', he cannot consistently announce in assembly, 'In order that school should function smoothly you must obey the following rules that the staff have devised as the best solution to such and such a problem.' Autonomy cannot be partial.

So it was that Countesthorpe from its start attracted a staff who felt that, to be consistent with its objectives, a traditional form of government from above was unacceptable. An executive administration was necessary, but policy was to be fashioned by mutual agreement among all concerned, rather than laid down by the headmaster and filtered down in a one-way process for implementation by staff and pupils. The sovereign body on fundamental decisions was to be by Moot, the gathering of staff, teaching and non-teaching, with participation by students on some evolving basis. The head had a voice, and was expected to be someone with telling experience and judgment, but he carried only one vote and no veto other than the threat of resignation.

This covers the main initial innovations at Countesthorpe. For the purposes of this paper I am making no reference to the very important fact that we are a Community College within the Leicestershire scheme. This is not because I undervalue the element of community education, but because this has not been the field of Countesthorpe's distinctive innovation so far. The innovations in community use of the college are in their infancy. The beginnings are there, in such features as adult students studying part-time for A levels alongside sixth-formers, and heavy use by a thousand or more people is made of separate clubs and classes. But in the sense that Andrew Fairbairn speaks of 'open access', the community college here is only just developing. Our peculiar contribution so far has been in what I have outlined – a statement of objectives and an attempt to achieve them by establishing curriculum, organization, learning style, staff-student relationships and a form of government that are consistent with them. What problems have arisen from them? What have been the main constraints?

Let me turn to certain implications in the stated objectives and the obstacles these predictably encountered. First, the recognition that a new understanding of student motivation was necessary and that this must come first. To the academic, learning provides its own motivation, the good student will be intrinsically self-motivated, and if only we provide sound teaching within a valid, relevant curriculum, the success generated will provide the stimulation for further learning. Establish the proper subject-disciplines, says this school, and good staff-student relationships will follow. This is attractive in as much as a bored student is a potential social problem, but it fails to recognize the extent to which adolescents in the 14–16 range will already have rejected conventional studies and the mistrust they will have built up towards the teacher who is dedicated to his subject but not interested in his students. Two dangers presented themselves. First the danger that teachers genuinely putting first their building of a trusting relationship were losing sight of its being a means and not an end in itself. They might thus fail to ask themselves whether the good relationship was leading to increased learning, albeit social as well as cognitive learning, and whether the relationship was a healthy one if it could not withstand, or even prosper from, reasonable demands as from teacher to student, or as from adult to adolescent. The second danger was consequent, and recurs frequently at other points of the innovation. Those adults in immediate contact from outside – parents, local government officers, tradesmen, police and teachers from neighbouring schools – reacted to novel forms of relationships between teachers and students by expressing anxiety, in forms ranging from scepticism to overt disapproval or even downright hostility.

This anxiety was usually over changes in external features, such as freedom of dress, use of first names for staff and so on. The more perceptive might notice the deeper problem arising from the second division of motivation. If you loosen the holds of classroom organization, arranging for mixed-ability groupings based on friendship patterns so as to reduce the dependence of motivation on pleasing teacher, you increase the motivating power of peer-group conformity. Thus a student, instead of choosing a particular line of work because he wants to please his teacher or because that work presents possibilities of being satisfying in itself, may opt for it because his mates are doing so. If that becomes his reason for opting in, it may well become his reason for opting out. And then the teacher is in a real dilemma, because he will have to persuade a close-knit group of anything he may be selling, and will find it a darn sight harder than selling it to the differentiated, if larger, group of the orthodox classroom. In addition, the teacher will often find that having stepped out of his dominant role, one or another of his students will step into it and we must then face the question of whether the new dominance is less desirable all round than the old one. There is no easy solution, but in an authoritarian situation such a transfer of power from class teacher to peer-group leader would be disastrous, leading inevitably to conflict. Within a participatory dispersal of power, however, where the Them-Us division is minimized, the situation is defused and becomes another basis for negotiation instead.

Looking next at objectives in terms of knowledge, there are certain implications. With the merging of certain areas of study, for instance into IG, the question will arise of whether students will be introduced to the variety of fields of knowledge through subject disciplines if they no longer appear as discrete specialisms, each with specialist teachers. This is the curriculum theorist's fear of a general mish-mash. And yet, below examination level, and even then now that the school-leaving age has been raised, the distinctive virtues of subject disciplines are unlikely to cut much ice with most pupils. David Layton, writing of pupils with average ability and below, maintained that 'learning undertaken in terms of the traditional disciplines is not easily made significant and relevant to the interests of these pupils. Such learning may be appropriate when pupils are selected by ability and high motivation. For others, something else is required. . . .' In fact, the boundaries of subjects were well enough understood by staff for differentiation to take place in time for 16 plus exams, but steps had to be taken to allay the fears of those parents who were predominantly exam-conscious and of students who arrived with well-formed habits of work along traditional lines of sequential stints of given tasks competitively assessed. If no one was regularly notching up their tasks against O level standard, they could lose their sense of direction and become demoralized. If passing an exam is one extrinsic motivating force, then one of our objectives under skills should be skill at passing exams. This applies equally well if the exams are largely in Mode III as ours have been, both GCE and CSE.

The biggest demands upon the teacher for revision of role arose from the objectives of problem-solving by hypothesis and from those associated with student autonomy. I have already indicated the likelihood of conflict between the fairly general public expectation of school maintaining the 'status quo' and the immediate noticeable results of participatory relationships between staff and students. By and large, society demands of the schools that they process children so as to produce docile and conformist employees. Lip service is paid to the virtues of initiative and interpretive skills, but it is always assumed that these will lead only to an ever more efficient society of the kind that we have got. If the interpretation leads to critical attack and the initiative to bids for radical change, then we soon hear that this is not what was looked for. One employer summed it up for me by saying, 'Can he spell? Will he do as he's told?'

But if our objective is to assist students to take increasing control of their own destinies, to question assumptions, to solve problems by being inventive and by being trained to envisage speculative alternatives, we are bound to meet conflict with an industrial society that sees school principally as the sorting house for employment. The opposition can take various forms, from the pressure put upon Youth Employment Officers by employers, to the demands by governors for the means of producing conformity within school: uniforms, assembly, gestures of respect and so on. In our own case, the suspicions have been directed principally at three main features: choice within curriculum, the non-authoritarian relationships of teachers and students and the participatory form of government. Even among those who have looked closely enough to realize that we have *not* just sold out to the students, that they do *not* do just as they please, that a continuous dialogue of guidance exists, there are many who will object because fundamentally the teachers are failing to dictate the fields of study, failing to instil a sense of respect for the respectable, failing to establish an institution whose form of government implies an unquestioning obedience to authority.

At Countesthorpe we are all engaged in this battle to win over local public opinion, though I think that as Principal I stand at the front of the phalanx. But simultaneously we are engaged internally with the problems that we find emerging in practice. The situation is never static: both our policies and our forms evolve continuously, lurching somewhat. Perhaps the first problem to emerge was the conflict between the provision for a balanced curriculum and the encouragement of student autonomy. Both objectives were teacher-given, yet they overestimated the likelihood of students accepting the equal value-weighing given to our six areas of curriculum. The principle of autonomy led us to timetable all students individually by a negotiation between student and staff, the result being open at any time to re-negotiation. This put staff in the position of selling the notion of balanced curriculum, but not surprisingly, the student, placed in the role of consumer, did not always buy. We accepted autonomy as the superordinating principle, but compromised by forging out a system which would eliminate the anarchy of lesson-refusal, or dropouts in full attendance.

A separate paper would be necessary to describe the solution devised for the start of the school's third year of running. Briefly though, it is organized around a series of staff triads, groups of three teachers with differing basic specialisms who have tutorial responsibility for ninety students and who teach them in core-time amounting (with variations) to half their timetable. This core-time will include English and Social Studies, plus another specialism derived from the third member of the triad. The other half of the timetable is constructed from the specialisms available elsewhere in school, sciences, languages, two- and three-dimensional arts, PE, maths. Some, particularly the potential candidates for HE will fill in many specialisms, but those taking on fewer, and those who underachieve because of the need for a build-up of security and confidence, fall back on the core-time teams. These teams work in large open areas of the building which thus become the home bases of their students, and the staff from the triads are there pretty well continuously to advise and direct their students. Thus no one drops out, but instead those less able to cope drop *in*, with the staff who know them best available to them. The system is highly flexible and has produced diversity that begins to look really comprehensive. It puts enormous demands upon core staff.

It is worth mentioning one problem subsequent upon our objective of devising a curriculum related to the student's needs and upon such organization as would implement this. The student's opportunity for negotiation among options leads to a fair degree of flitting, at least initially. Unless the student has already internalized the discipline of deferred satisfactions, interest may wane and a subject be dropped. Of course, the core-tutor will not at once conclude that the subject is now dead for such a student, and will in time encourage a renewed interest and return to it. But he will seek for something that arouses interest in the student as an alternative to whatever it is that has been rejected. Two dangers lie in this. One is the possibility that the student will fail to persist, and not learn what can be achieved with delayed goals. The other is the possibility that the teacher taking upon himself the responsibility for the all-important motivation of his students, and straining after interesting and exciting subject material and work schemes, will eat his heart out with guilt as the student remains uninterested and unexcited. Fortunately, human nature usually asserts itself in a teacher, who eventually tends to say, 'I have made a dozen suggestions: unless you have a better one, you must take up one of mine.'

Another paradox has been that a highly innovatory situation has called for a predominantly young staff, not settled into styles of work that would be difficult to change, without too much at stake in terms of status, well endowed with stamina. Yet by the same token they are lacking in experience and open to being taken advantage of by adolescents recently moved from a more traditional discipline. New staff accept that status and respect are to be acquired rather than conferred from above, but students accustomed to teachers who demand respect by virtue of their role as teachers, will often at first be confused by the absence of external controls, and work off their previously restrained reactions on their new and more permissive teachers. This, in turn, produces rapid reaction from parents, officialdom and the various bystanders who find confirmation of their worst fears, of original sin asserting itself in the absence of concerted repression. Wilful damage, noise, time-wasting, lack of conventional deferences to authority-figures were not difficult to find in the opening terms, and those who expected school to conform to the known patterns were not slow in drawing attention to them. The conditions themselves improved much more speedily than the local attitudes. Time has been the crucial factor, and we are still fighting for time. Time can bring experience to the inexperienced and it has also enabled our original students to take in the opportunities of our system and forget about reacting to its novelty. But a number of scars will take time to fade.

This leaves us with the problems of a participatory government. We operate something quite different from a consultative government. Schools are increasingly offering advisory consultation to teachers and students, but this remains essentially an arrangement of advise and consent for both those parties, while the head, perhaps with some form of cabinet, consults and decides. Teachers may advise on curriculum, but usually the students' sphere of consultation is limited to domestic issues. We, on the other hand, see participation as real joint policy making, agreement by consensus, with curriculum and domestic issues inseparable. All those concerned with what takes place in the college are involved in the decision-making Moot. But how are these identified? Initially it was all staff, teaching and non-teaching, (including clerical, ancillary and caretaking staff), and students in fifth and sixth forms. No decisions were acceptable without reasonable consensus, or if a confrontation arose between blocks, say of staff against students. In fact, the early terms revealed no tendency towards such divisions, and over three years the Moot has been extended to the fourth year and to parents. Having been given the option, few students or parents take part, though the growth of sixth form is bringing an increase of regular attenders. The problem still remains of who may reasonably expect to have a voice in the Moot. If students, what about ex-students who continue as part-time adult students? If parents, what about local residents, ratepayers and employers? This has hardly been faced.

Is the possible tyranny of a head worse than possible tyranny of the demagogic debater or filibusterer? The fear of an articulate minority gaining power without public accountability has often been expressed to me, and it may well be a hypothetical danger. But the real safeguard has to date been a staff attracted by the opportunity of openly negotiated policy. A staff of inarticulate conformists would soon be prey to the first opportunists moving into the power vacuum, but this has not been the situation. What has happened is that a small minority found that in practice they could not tolerate open negotiation and the need to justify the actions they advocated. Some could not bear the clash and conflict inevitably entailed. They were unhappy without the support of a hierarchy by which they could be given a directive from above or an authority to quote, and so they left. Those remaining tend to be readier for contention, which is hopeful when we look towards continuous innovation. There remains, however, the problem of appointing staff, especially older men and women, whose commitment in action and under stress will remain congruent with their doctrine, who will be able to live with, support and develop the work patterns that emerge as a result of beliefs held and expressed in all honesty at the time of interview. We have found it crucial to observe applicants for a period, if only for a day, while exposed to school and in contact with the students. Significantly, several probationer entrants to staff have become known to us during their teaching practice periods here. It is not so easy to learn in advance how experienced teachers are going to behave.

In the early months, the deliberations of the Moot consumed time greedily when it might have been devoted to out-of-hours student activities in a structure less open to debate. Once a body of policy had been hammered out, however, meetings became less frequent and have levelled off to about one a month. Fewer issues arising were deemed to be fundamental: more of them involved intermediate decisions in the light of past Moot decisions. The question has increasingly become one of effective executive action. Without jeopardizing the principle of corporate responsibility, how few people need to be involved in the making of a decision? Our tendency at first, with all meetings advertised and open to all, was for full debate in which everyone had a say. Increasingly, as business has mounted, smaller executive or advisory groups were set up to sift information and opinion so as to formulate proposals. Even this need to refer back to the parent body for ratification proved cumbersome, but there were those who found it hard to accept that it was not necessarily undemocratic if some decisions were reached without everyone being party to them. The Moot is there for final appeal, but on some highly contentious issues, such as appointments to staff and distribution of allowances, the Moot has itself decided to delegate decision to an elected group empowered to act without further reference except in the event of deadlock.

If the final decision and arbitration rests with the Moot, what remains for the Principal except executive action? Is he reduced to the position of lift attendant in a bungalow? I find rather that he exists as the hinge in the nutcracker, a position of some strain, standing between the school, where he is accountable to the Moot, and the administration, where he is accountable to the local authority and the governors. The crux of the matter, the validation of putting one's head between the lion's jaws like this, is that while initiative and innovation may now flow in from any point of origin, staff or student, the Principal, with both long experience of school development and knowledge of the workings of the administrators, public and parent bodies, and so on, can advise and influence. He can say, with more certainty than anyone else on staff, what reaction may be expected from outside and how it may best be dealt with. He can also warn when reaction may become intolerable for him personally since he has to speak for and answer for all that happens in the name of the school. So just as he abandons any veto on Moot decisions, the Moot avoids action that would make his position impossible by requiring his defence of something he found fundamentally abhorrent. Moot and Principal must be in agreement on the deepest issues.

Nevertheless a vast gap exists between the democratically structured school where authority is corporate, where initiative may have innumerable sources, and the expectation of parents, police and local government officers, who are accustomed to autocratic headship where to command is to be obeyed. The gap is particularly uncomfortable when there is a crisis and the Principal is expected to solve it by swift decision and a show of authority. ('I'm sure if you just told them . . .'). A long job of public explanation is taking place, but at the same time the Principal is the person most readily available to the outside when the overall view is called for, when a stand needs to be made. He is not sole spokesman, but he is the one asked for as often as not, whether by the Chairman of the Education Committee, the press, or a conference wanting a paper such as this one.

The main concern expressed in the previous paper was that of maintaining innovation. Indeed, now that the need for change is becoming more generally accepted, this is the major problem facing schools. As our institutions are at present structured, innovation is most likely to be introduced from without, as from a Schools Council project or the arrival of a new head. In this, some theorists are right. But if the institution is restructured so that communication is multi-directional and authority is corporate then two things begin to happen. First, the school will attract teachers who want to initiate and want to collaborate. Second, the knowledge of bearing responsibility for what happens, instead of being able to pass the buck up the hierarchy, forces such teachers to make things work, to rethink, to adapt. They are highly motivated to innovate because they have formulated objectives, they have made policies, they have chosen the colleagues with whom to work, so it had damned well better work.

And this, in practice, is what we have found. There is a fecundity of ideas and a situation of acceptable conflict which ensures that a critical selection ensues. The abrasion is essential. Nothing is more alien to innovation than the flabbiness of 'a happy staffroom'. In any stage of our curriculum development, up to half a dozen young teachers are likely to formulate thought-out schemes, each worthy of the mind of a single Director of Studies. Then there is argument and the Principal's job is no longer to pour oil on the troubled water but to fish in them.

The other and parallel source of innovation, hardly tapped as yet, is the demand of the school student. Our first sixth is hardly six months old, and we are bottom-heavy for another year with high school children (11–13). Increasingly we shall hear the voice of the student with clear views about curriculum and organization. The student, sometimes still echoing the parent, but often in conflict with home, will want to shape the objectives, not just participate in deciding the means by which they may be achieved. The very structure of schools and the force of tradition in what Margaret Mead identified as a post-figurative culture, usually prevents the student source of innovation from flowing. We have the structures to allow and encourage this source to well up, and there is every reason to believe that over the next two or three years it will do so.

There is no problem about innovation being maintained: the real challenge in our situation is to ensure that innovation takes direction from the agreed objectives. If we can maintain this sense of direction then we can avoid what Alvin Toffler recently referred to as talking of innovation when what we really meant was 'making the system more effective at carrying out obsolete goals.' It remains for everyone involved at Countesthorpe to have enough faith in the future to let it, and not the past, determine the present.

My final question asks whether the Countesthorpe model could be adopted by other schools. That remains to be seen, but I would not advocate it unless two conditions are guaranteed: first, a local authority supportive of the venture, and second, opportunity to appoint initial staff eager to subscribe to stated, shared objectives and willing to carry the work-loads and responsibilities that follow from participatory government. To attempt an imitation in an existing school would be disastrous. So we do not offer a blueprint to many, but rather a demonstration that alternatives can be pursued, that objectives are worth formulating, that students and assistant teachers can themselves generate and maintain change without total dependence on initiative from above and without. It is then up to others to translate these hopes into particular local practices.